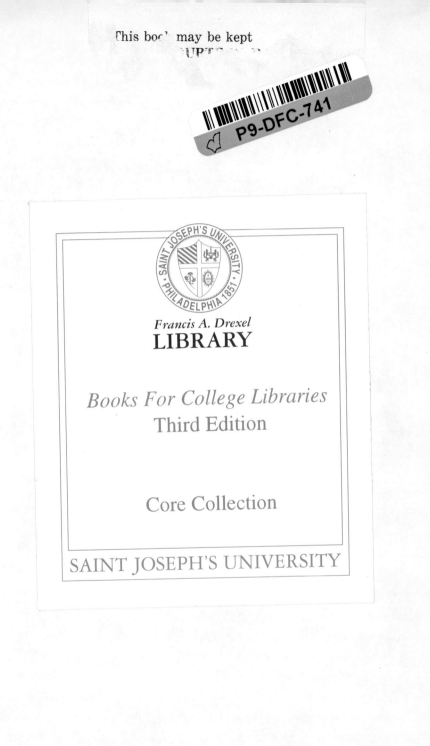

The Open Door College

A CASE STUDY

THE CARNEGIE SERIES IN AMERICAN EDUCATION

The books in this series have resulted from studies supported by grants of the Carnegie Corporation of New York, and are published by McGraw-Hill in recognition of their importance to the future of American education.

The Corporation, a philanthropic foundation established in 1911 by Andrew Carnegie for the advancement and diffusion of knowledge and understanding, has a continuing interest in the improvement of American education. It financed the studies in this series to provide facts and recommendations which would be useful to all those who make or influence the decisions which shape American educational policies and institutions.

The statements made and views expressed in these books are solely the responsibility of the authors.

Books Published

CLARK · The Open Door College: A Case Study
CONANT · The American High School Today
GLENNY · Autonomy of Public Colleges
PIERSON · The Education of American Businessmen

In Preparation

HENNINGER · The Technical Institute in America
MEDSKER · The Junior College: Progress and Prospect

The Open Door College

A CASE STUDY

Burton R. Clark

CENTER FOR THE STUDY OF HIGHER EDUCATION
UNIVERSITY OF CALIFORNIA (BERKELEY)

McGRAW-HILL BOOK COMPANY, INC.

New York Toronto London 1960

 Library of Congress Catalog Card Number 59-14440

11140

II

To My Parents

A new institution, the junior college, has sprung up in large numbers to meet the demand for something like mass education beyond the normal four-year secondary school. . . . It is in many ways a transitional institution. Its courses of study have the qualities of both secondary and higher education. . . . Over the years its relationship to higher education will become clearer, but the junior college will, in all probability, borrow more than it will contribute to the quality of higher education.

Richard Hofstadter and C. DeWitt Hardy, *The Development and Scope of Higher Education in the United States,* Columbia University Press, New York, 1952, pp. 141–142.

As the junior college movement spreads, we may see many twilight colleges, which appear free from the perspective of the high school but almost unprotected and even obscurantist from the perspective of the traditional private college. And at many of these junior colleges, as at some of the state or poorer private institutions, the chief academic freedom issues that arise do not involve ideas or associations, but rather the right of professors to flunk students who are plainly inadequate but who arguably may gain from postponing their entry on the job market.

David Riesman, *Constraint and Variety in American Education,* University of Nebraska Press, Lincoln, Nebr., 1956, p. 123.

The lesson is this: Those who deal with the more obvious ideals—such as education, science, creativity, or freedom—should more fully recognize the dependence of these ideals on congenial though often mundane administrative arrangements.

Philip Selznick, *Leadership in Administration: A Sociological Interpretation,* Row, Peterson & Company, Evanston, Ill., 1957, p. 141.

Foreword

The junior college has an ambiguous status in the American educational system. Legally, it is usually defined as a part of secondary education, and organizationally, it may be part of a unified school district that also operates one or more elementary schools and high schools. In any event, it is ordinarily the creature of a *local* district with all the overtones this location supplies.

In effect, however, the junior college is a part of the enterprise of higher education. Its students are counted in the statistics of enrollment in higher institutions. In the country at large about one-fourth, and in California one-half, the total college enrollment is found in junior colleges. The curriculum which carries the most prestige in these institutions is that which parallels the first two years of four-year colleges and universities. And, in general, two-thirds of junior college students are in transfer curricula, although only about one-third of them actually will transfer to senior colleges.

This indeterminate status is only one of the factors that make it especially difficult for a junior college to attain a clear identity; to create in the minds of students, faculty, parents, and community a distinct image; and to define its role clearly and realistically.

The multiple functions that the junior college is expected to perform also confuse and blur the image. The transfer curriculum identifies the junior college with four-year institutions, institutions that may be geographically remote. The terminal vocational curricula identify the junior college with essential local concerns, particularly local industries and homely pursuits. Thus its sanctions are various, and they come from different sources. On the one hand, the work of the college is evaluated by the success of its graduates in four-year institutions, and, on the other hand, its work is appraised by the quality of personnel it supplies for local business and industry. These sanctions carry different orders of prestige to various groups both inside and outside the college. The disparity makes organizational unity and distinctiveness difficult to attain.

The diversity of the typical junior college student body also contributes to the blurring of status and role. Many junior colleges have an open-door admission policy which brings them a cross section of the community; this means a heavy concentration from lower socioeconomic groups compared with most other colleges. The distribution of students' scholastic-aptitude-test scores may also be skewed toward the lower levels. Thus the junior college, like the comprehensive high school, is supposed to serve students with widely varying interests, abilities, and cultural backgrounds; this is a difficult task at best, but it is an especially complicated problem when the staff must remember that in the long run the reputation of the college will probably depend on its success in preparing a relatively small proportion of its students for senior college work.

Reference has already been made to the fact that, over-all, about two-thirds of the students in junior colleges are in transfer curricula but that only about one-third of them go on to four-year institutions. Those who are classified or self-classified as transfer students but who do not transfer, Dr. Clark calls the "latent terminals." The aspirations of these students are supported by strong social forces in the American culture. Dr. Clark points out that the handling of the large number of latent or concealed terminals is a problem with wide social implications. He has discussed the ways in which the junior college performs what he calls "the cooling-out function" and has explained how the community college is able to do this more effectively, so far as the students' attitudes and educational alternatives are concerned, than the four-year institution.

Dr. Clark has pointed out, however, that this cooling-out function needs to be disguised, for if it becomes obvious, the ability of the junior college to perform it is impaired. But this covert process in itself impedes the development of a precise image and a clearly defined role. Nevertheless, it is a process which, as Dr. Clark observes, goes far in enabling American higher education to be both democratic and selective.

Dr. Clark has highlighted the factors that determine the character of a junior college by making an intensive case study of the development of the San Jose Junior College in California. This institution shares with many other junior colleges the conditions that make the attainment of legitimation difficult. But the college in its relatively short history has had to cope with a set of environmental factors which, while they are not different in kind from the forces sketched above, are peculiar enough to illuminate, in an emphatic way, the problem of achieving an organizational identity and role.

The San Jose case study is an application to an important type of educational organization of the methods of institutional analysis. This sort of analysis represents a broad concern with the character of organizations and particularly with the ways in which dominant patterns of organization take form in interaction with internal and external environments. The intent is to study characteristics of organizations in their own right, the characteristics of "whole organizations" or major components thereof. Individual roles, the behavior of small groups, and minor structures are studied only as they may be shown to influence or reflect general organizational character. As Selznick has said, "Institutional analysis asks the question: What is the bearing of an existing or proposed procedure on the distinctive role and character of the enterprise?" [1]

There is insufficient space here to list all the antecedents of present-day interest in institutional analysis. But it may be noted that this interest stems in considerable part from Max Weber's classic statement of the characteristics of bureaucratic and large-scale organization in industrial society. The writings of Chester I. Barnard and Herbert A. Simon on organizational structure and administrative behavior have also stimulated the development of methods of institutional analysis. Robert K. Merton, Alvin W. Gouldner, Peter Blau, and especially Philip Selznick have made significant contributions to the study of organizations as organizations.

There is a growing interest in the identification and description of college atmospheres, and it has been suggested that some institutions, particularly certain small colleges, have developed distinctive climates. Dr. C. Robert Pace and his associates have approached the description of college environments as a whole by the use of an index of college characteristics, "which consists of statements of activities, policies, procedures, attitudes, and impressions which might be characteristic of various colleges. . . . The statements in the test are indicative of environmental presses which are judged to correspond to certain personality needs." [2]

[1] Philip Selznick, *Leadership in Administration: A Sociological Interpretation*, Row, Peterson & Company, Evanston, Ill., 1957, p. 140.

[2] C. R. Pace and G. G. Stern, *A Criterion Study of College Environment*, Psychological Research Center, Syracuse University Research Institute. Syracuse, N.Y., 1958, p. 8.

Institutional analysis is another and perhaps complementary approach to the characterization of "environment-as-a-whole." It bids well to serve as a powerful tool in describing the organizational character of a college, in revealing differences among institutions in pervasive climate or atmosphere and, ultimately, in assessing the impact of a college on students of known characteristics. The method is being put to use by Dr. Clark and others in the five-year study now under way at the Center for the Study of Higher Education on institutional distinctiveness and institutional impact in a group of selected colleges. The results of these studies and of the study reported in this volume should make an important contribution to both sociological and educational theory and practice.

T. R. McConnell, Chairman

CENTER FOR THE STUDY OF
HIGHER EDUCATION,
UNIVERSITY OF CALIFORNIA,
BERKELEY, CALIFORNIA

Acknowledgments

This study was assisted by several organizations. The Pacific Southwest Center (Stanford University) of the Kellogg Cooperative Program in Educational Administration supported an exploratory phase of the research in the summer and fall of 1955, while I was on the Stanford faculty. The Harvard Graduate School of Education, while I was a staff member there, encouraged the completion of the research and assisted in the preparation of an early draft of this report. The Center for the Study of Higher Education, University of California (Berkeley), aided the later stages of the field research and also subsidized the analysis and final writing. I am especially indebted to T. R. McConnell, chairman of the center, for the encouragement which he has given the study and for the foreword he has contributed to this book.

This study could hardly have been made without the cooperation of the organizations studied. San Jose Junior College and the San Jose Unified School District provided access to their personnel, records, and internal affairs. Many individual members of these organizations gave generously of their time and knowledge, and they go unnamed here only to protect their anonymity. I am indebted especially to the officials of the college and the district and earnestly hope this study will in some measure add to the understanding of their own concerns.

For advice and assistance in various phases of the work I am grateful to Herbert Maccoby, Leland L. Medsker, Sheldon Messinger, David Nasatir, and Martin A. Trow. Special acknowledgment goes to Philip Selznick for the analytical framework used in this study. My use of his ideas will be apparent throughout the following pages.

Burton R. Clark

Contents

Introduction

Education is one of the major American institutions whose organized life has remained largely unanalyzed. A sizable body of knowledge exists now about the business firm, the government bureau, the trade union, the hospital, the political party, and special private associations. In comparison, the church and the school have received little systematic study. In education an enormous number of agencies exists, public and private, from the nursery school to the university, which affect the quality of American life. The schools and colleges of the country transmit the general culture, train the young, and nourish (or deplete) basic social values. These broad functions are variously performed, according to the way in which the schools are shaped by their tasks, the social trends in their area, and the administrative systems of which they are a part. A comprehension of the forms that modern educational organizations are assuming would be useful for a better understanding of educational problems as well as for a general theory of organizations. This book is intended as a contribution to this aim.

Much of the light shed on organizations by recent studies has stemmed from a willingness to see organizations as systems in their own right. The perspective of this study is different from, although it may overlap with or utilize, perspectives that emphasize the psychology of leadership, the performance of individuals in roles, and the behavior of members of small groups. Free of the tendency to reduce all social phenomena to the level of individual action, this perspective takes the whole organization as the unit for study. The view is taken here that an organization develops an identifiable character and takes on roles in the larger society. Individuals, small groups, and divisions of an organization enter into view only for the purpose of describing what an organization as an entity is like, how it behaves, and what tasks it is able to perform. This study attempts to delineate the character of a junior college, show how this character was determined, and indicate its consequences.

To assess the nature of an organization systematically and in detail an intensive case analysis is necessary. The research on which this report is based took the form of a case study. A number of interrelated activities needed to be seen in connection with one another. This could hardly have been done by surveying a large number of organizations on a few selected characteristics or, for that matter, by using a single technique for gathering information. Information was gained through informal interviews, analysis of documents, and a questionnaire. But by no means was the case study made for the case itself. It was meant to identify conditions and consequences that are, in part at least, evident elsewhere. Comparative data and comparisons of characteristics of other types of schools about which much is already known are used to generalize about a *type* of educational organization.

The case study concerns a two-year college in California. The junior college is a school whose place in education is by no means clear and whose character has been problematic. Not yet fixed in the American educational system—in some states it does not exist—the public junior college is more of an educational unknown than the elementary school, the high school, the private liberal arts college, the state college, and the university. Its newness renders it especially interesting for organizational study. An organization in an established field may assume a character through routine adoption of an established pattern; several well-worn paths will be open to it and there may be little that is problematic. Such may be the case today of an average elementary school or perhaps a dental college. But in less well-established fields, an organization makes its way more on its own, subject to the push and pull of environment and perhaps without clear-cut models to imitate. Outsiders are likely to be found lacking in information about its practices and holding contradictory images. To study a junior college was to increase the likelihood of finding an illuminating situation in which the character of an organization is formed by interaction with its environment. It is also plausible that organizations in recently formed fields will be more likely to reflect present tendencies of society than will organizations whose character was originally formed in past eras. The junior college has something to tell us about the pressures of modern society on education.

The public junior college is entirely a twentieth-century phenomenon. None existed at the turn of the century; nineteen units that could be considered public junior colleges were in existence by 1915, but their total enrollment did not exceed 600 students. Rapid growth occurred after World War I; there were 178 colleges with 45,000 students by 1930, 261 colleges with 168,000 students in 1940, and 329 schools with more than 450,000 students in 1950.[1] One unbroken trend throughout this

[1] *Junior College Directory, 1957,* American Association of Junior Colleges, Washington, D.C. After 1940, junior college enrollment figures included large numbers of part-time special and adult students. By 1950, this category was more than 50 per cent of total reported enrollment. Even so, public junior colleges accounted for about one-third the enrollment of full-time entering students in all public colleges and universities in 1958. See Leland L. Medsker, *The Junior College: Progress and Prospect,* McGraw-Hill Book Company, Inc., New York, 1960, chap. 1.

time was the increasing numerical dominance of the public over the private junior college; by 1957, 85 per cent of all junior college students were enrolled in the public units.[2] The "junior college movement" has become largely a public venture and will become more so during the next decades.

The public junior college has developed unevenly within states and regions of the country: its spread varies from near absence in New England to a heavy concentration in California. The sixty colleges of the California system had approximately 250,000 full-time and part-time students in 1950, or more than 50 per cent of the nation's junior college enrollment; at the same time only eight other states had more than 10,000 students: New York, Illinois, Michigan, Texas, Missouri, Georgia, Mississippi, and Washington.

In California, public education generally has long been well supported. As to the rise of junior colleges, the state passed legislation in 1907, the earliest in the country, permitting the establishing of postgraduate programs attached to high schools, and began in 1917 to offer state aid for the support of the thirteenth and fourteenth years at a level comparable with the lower grades. From the beginning these grades were tuition-free. Considerable expansion took place during the 1920s and by 1930 thirty-five colleges were in operation. These early colleges attempted chiefly to parallel the work of the first two years in the university and four-year college, preparing students to transfer to the senior colleges in their junior year. The legislation of 1907 specified, in fact, that junior college "courses of studies shall approximate the studies prescribed in the first two years of University courses," [3] and as new colleges were established, they were generally committed to college preparation. For example, San

[2] *Higher Education,* U.S. Department of Health, Education, and Welfare, vol. 14, no. 5, p. 76, January, 1958.

[3] Quoted in H. A. Spindt, "Beginnings of the Junior College in California, 1907–1921," *College and University,* vol. 33, no. 1, pp. 22–28, fall, 1957.

Bernardino Valley College, established in 1926, had at the time of its founding the paramount aim of offering a curriculum comparable with the lower-division work of the University of California.[4] Until the middle of the 1920s, there was relatively little consideration of other operations. But from that point on the junior colleges became more complex, claiming "functions" that related to students who would not transfer. During the 1930s, "terminal" programs came to be seen as a unique effort of the junior college and acquired importance in junior college doctrine. During and following World War II, junior colleges embraced adult education and related activities for part-time students as a third major activity, to the extent that there were commonly more part-time than full-time students. The trend has been toward comprehensiveness, and in the past decade, these multiple-purpose colleges have increasingly referred to themselves as "community colleges."

The growth of the California junior college made it an important part of the state's system of higher education, the state university and the state college being the other major segments. Control and administration of the junior college, however, differs from that of the other two forms. The branches of the University of California, of which there were eight at the time the research for this study was concluded (1957), are governed by a single board of regents that is an independent unit of state government. The state colleges, numbering ten in 1957, have a different governing board, the state board of education, which is also statewide. The sixty-odd junior colleges, in contrast, are a part of local school government, falling under diversely located boards of education. In their constitutional position, the junior colleges are a part of the public schools and are, in fact, legally defined as secondary schools.[5] California does not have public junior col-

[4] Elbert K. Fretwell, Jr., *Founding Public Junior Colleges*, Bureau of Publications, Teachers College, Columbia University, New York, 1954, p. 53.

[5] State of California Education Code, Sacramento, 1955, sec. 8702.

leges under any other form of educational authority, such as the university, the state board of education (directly), or independent state bodies.

Legally a part of the public schools but educationally a part of higher education, a number of alternative orientations seem possible for this form of college organization. It could become similar to the four-year college in outlook, assume practices similar to those of the high school, or perhaps emerge as a hybrid with college and public school characteristics. It could also be fundamentally unlike any of the better-known forms. The first alternative—that the junior college is simply the first two years of college, a lower-division version of a liberal arts college—appears as a widespread public impression. The second possibility is reflected in the belief of some educators and laymen that the junior college is too often a polite name for several more years of high school. The third and fourth possibilities are generally offered by junior college spokesmen, with uniqueness claimed in the sense of either a new amalgamation or a completely new orientation. The executive secretary of the American Association of Junior Colleges has stated that the public junior college is "neither the upward extension of secondary education, nor the arm of the senior institution, nor the tail of a four-year college." In this view, "these colleges can be and often are operated under the public school system without being secondary in character of program, methods, and objectives." [6]

These alternatives pose the question of what kind of character the public junior college tends to assume. Inquiry based on this question and centered on a California college has more than local significance; not only is California leading in the junior college movement, but its form of junior college government is also found in other states. In the country as a whole, more than three-fourths of the public two-year colleges are administered

[6] *American Junior Colleges,* 4th ed., American Council on Education, Washington, D.C., 1956, p. 41.

by forms of local school government. It is safe to predict that the junior college will assume a larger place in American education during the next half century. As it does so, forms of local control promise to be nationally decisive. At least, control by the local public schools will be *the* major alternative to control by the university or the state.

In selecting a junior college for intensive observation, it was decided to study one that had been established only recently. A new organization would be in the process of assuming its initial structure and outlook. Its early history would be in the making, offering an opportunity to find the determinants of an emerging character in features of the present-day scene. This situation had certain advantages over the study of a mature school, where current orientation might be a product of a dimly remembered past and poorly recorded developments. The disadvantage in selecting a new institution was the risk of premature analysis, of completing a study before trends were manifested and while character was yet in doubt. The present analysis is based on only the first four years of existence of San Jose Junior College. But, as will be seen, this college had certain inescapable commitments that were early apparent, and stemming from these were durable consequences. Definite characterological tendencies could be seen and their persistence predicted for the future, barring a radical shift in the administrative setting. In such matters, the evidence, of course, is never all in; at no point, early or late, is the nature of an organization irrevocably fixed. What can be studied at any one time are the ways in which an organization is formed and transformed by internal and external pressures.

The study is presented as follows: The first chapter discusses the administrative setting in which San Jose Junior College is placed and some of the resulting problems. The college had great difficulty in becoming embedded in its area, because it was a new college in a relatively new movement and because it had to make its way in a web of organization which was somewhat unfavorable to it. Central here are the implications of location in a local school district. Chapter 2 concentrates on the student clientele of the college as it is shaped by admission policy. Highlighted is the way in which the wishes of the students affected the purpose and outlook of the college; a central problem of the public junior college is identified. In Chapter 3, further effects of the administrative setting and the student clientele are traced in the evolution of a formal organizational structure, the composition and orientation of the administrative staff, and the building of an appropriate instructional force. The empirical materials of these three chapters are used in Chapter 4 as a basis for describing and interpreting organization character. The college is seen to be heavily dependent and oriented toward a secondary school model of organization. The junior college is posed as a kind of mass enterprise and problems of this type of college are analyzed. Chapter 5 sets forth certain roles in higher education that the junior college performs, concentrating on a latent role that is involved in its special nature. Methodological explanations are found in the appendixes.

CHAPTER I

The Administrative Web

The environment of a new organization is shaped by many features of the larger society, such as traditional beliefs, established systems of authority, and the prerogatives of other organizations. In a general sense all formal enterprises are part of a larger social structure. For some, however, the connection between organization and setting is intimate and compelling while for others it is loose and remotely constraining. A close connection is likely to exist for an organization that is made part of a larger administrative complex. The host organization is a miniature society in itself, spelling out many of the ways in which things should be done. The history and character of the larger enterprise attach to the new organization, and certain expectations and procedures are automatically brought to bear. In such settings, location is important because it fixes a place for the new work group in a well-defined context.

Public schools and colleges are nearly always parts of a larger complex. Junior colleges are made part of a university or of a local public school system or, when separately established, of a state system. These alternative administrative systems cast the junior college in different molds. The local school system is the most frequently found context of public junior colleges. What are the consequences for the junior college if it is controlled by the local schools? Some consequences found in San Jose appear unique or uncommon, resulting from conditions not to be expected elsewhere; but San Jose also possesses conditions that are found widely elsewhere, and case analysis can serve to suggest common effects. The public schools provide a general type of administrative web. The following account of the place of San Jose Junior College suggests consequences of this particular kind of setting for the character of colleges.

THE ANTECEDENT PROGRAM

The newly established junior college in the city of San Jose had had, by 1953, a long prenatal existence. Its conception dated from 1921 when certain courses of study were prescribed by the Board of Education of San Jose and "declared to constitute the junior college department of the San Jose High School."[1] Although legally part of a high school, these courses were to be maintained by the San Jose State Teachers College (which later became San Jose State College) under contract with the local schools.[2] This contractual arrangement was maintained until 1953, with the junior college operation housed and administered by the state college throughout this extended period. Meanwhile the program underwent several changes in its legal standing. A separate junior college district, one however that was coterminous with the boundaries of the San Jose high school district and administered by the same school board, was formed in 1928, and the cluster of courses formerly declared to be a high school department was renamed the "San Jose Junior College."[3] This separate-district status ended in 1936 when the junior college district was merged into a newly created San Jose Unified School District along with the elementary schools and high schools of

[1] San Jose Unified School District, Minutes of the Board of Education, Nov. 22, 1921.

[2] *Ibid.*

[3] *Ibid.*, Sept. 11, 1928.

the city. Again, the controlling board remained operationally the same. The import of the 1936 integration of districts was that the unified-district form of school government became fixed in San Jose and has ever since been the constitutional framework for the college. This framework became an administrative setting when the college was separated from state college administration.

The legal identity which the college had at all times between 1921 and 1953 did not mean, however, that it had organizational life. It was in practice a virtually indistinguishable part of the administration of San Jose State College. The president of the state college was considered its chief administrative agent, having such titles as president and principal of the junior college.[4] Teachers assigned to this operation on the state college campus appeared in the financial records of the school district as instructor, assistant professor, associate professor, and professor with pay fixed accordingly.[5] They were actually state college personnel, paid by the public schools. Persons who had at one time been assigned to the junior college payroll in this fashion reported when interviewed that they had always thought of themselves as part of the state college staff. Both colleges operated in the same physical plant, and the student bodies were largely fused. Students were designated as belonging to the junior college or the state college at the discretion of state college authorities. Classified as "junior college" were students who planned to terminate their education in one or two years and four-year students with a low academic performance.[6] Junior college and

[4] *Ibid.*, May 5, 1928 and July 22, 1947.

[5] *Ibid.*, July 22, 1947.

[6] Put more formally: "At San Jose [State College] six units with A or B grades [high school] are required for 'clear standing'; other students enroll in the junior college, with opportunity to transfer to the state college if their scholarship warrants." *A Report of a Survey of the Needs of California in Higher Education*, Committee on the Conduct of the Study of Higher Education in California, Sacramento, 1948, pp. 34–35; hereinafter cited as *Report of Survey*.

state college students, mixing in classes, were outwardly indistinguishable. And since the assignment of students was largely a matter of designation in the records, it was not necessary for a student to be aware that he was other than in the senior organization. The place of the junior college operation was approximately that of a submerged extension division.

The junior college was thus chiefly a bookkeeping and financial transaction,[7] and as such it was advantageous for both the San Jose district and the state college. A considerable financial benefit accrued to the district, a fact that later colored the reception given the separate college of 1953. The district's annual bill from the state college for the running of the junior college operation was largely covered by income received from state aid for junior colleges and from tuition paid to the district by other districts that were sending students to the junior college. These two sources commonly covered from 70 to 100 per cent of the expense.[8] The district also collected a local junior college tax, which it was then able to use for other purposes.[9]

> Of the \$.35 per \$100 [of assessed valuation] authorized by the educational code for Junior College purposes, only \$.04 per

[7] This has been a common pattern in California where a junior college has been administered by a state college. On two similar cases, a state study reported: "Junior college students are not distinguishable from state-college students unless they declare terminal objectives or unless they are ineligible for admission to one of the four-year curriculums. Junior-college students are enrolled in the same courses with state-college students. . . . Thus, in effect, the terminal program exists on paper only, since the so-called terminal-vocational curriculums are put together from a pool of regular state-college courses." *A Restudy of the Needs of California in Higher Education,* California State Department of Education, Sacramento, 1955, p. 61; hereinafter cited as *Restudy.*

[8] See Table 2 for the last three years of state college administration (1950–1951, 1951–1952, and 1952–1953).

[9] "Let's Look at Local Government," *Report Submitted to the Board of Education by the Santa Clara County Taxpayers' Association,* San Jose Unified School District, Minutes of the Board of Education, Nov. 20, 1952.

> year of tax money has been given to State College to program and administer. This low Junior College tax cost enabled the San Jose Unified School District to implement and heighten its high school and elementary school programs.

With about 11 per cent of this money going to the junior college, nearly 90 per cent went to other uses. This way of running a junior college operation was thus both inexpensive and rewarding to other school personnel, virtues that did not escape the eyes of tax groups, administrators, and teachers in the schools. As for the state college side of this arrangement:[10]

> San Jose State College has been able to use the $300,000 plus dollars it received each year from the San Jose District to its best advantage. If the State College was refused on some part of its program by the State Department of Education, college officials could fall back on the San Jose money to further the program vetoed by State Officials. By the exercising of certain economies due to an increased enrollment above a pure State College, it could do this and still provide an adequate Junior College program.

The size of this junior college operation compared with the total size of the state college can be seen in enrollment figures. Table 1 shows the junior college share of the total student body of the state college campus from 1929 to 1953. As can be seen in the last column of the table, the junior college was assigned more than 30 per cent of the students on campus until 1942. Between 1941 and 1942, the junior college enrollment fell off drastically while the state college increased in size, and from 1942 to 1944 the junior college share was half of what it was before. Between 1944 and 1945, its share of students was doubled and during the immediate postwar years remained near this level. A tapering-off after 1948 then produced a picture similar to that of the World War II period. These extensive and some-

[10] *Ibid.*

Table 1

Annual Enrollment of San Jose State College and San Jose Junior College, 1929–1953

Year ending	Total	State college	Junior college	
			Number	Per cent of total
1929	2,009	1,293	716	36
1930	2,215	1,509	706	32
1931	2,609	1,807	802	31
1932	2,875	1,943	932	32
1933	2,979	1,950	1,029	34
1934	2,822	1,781	1,041	37
1935	3,136	1,929	1,207	38
1936	3,132	1,923	1,209	39
1937	3,315	1,926	1,389	42
1938	3,527	2,099	1,428	40
1939	3,879	2,334	1,545	40
1940	4,449	2,754	1,695	38
1941	4,554	2,933	1,621	35
1942	3,901	3,264	637	16
1943	2,933	2,505	428	15
1944	1,906	1,663	243	13
1945	2,310	1,616	694	30
1946	4,326	3,212	1,114	26
1947	6,865	4,930	1,935	28
1948	7,780	5,664	2,116	27
1949	8,344	6,596	1,748	21
1950	8,839	7,548	1,291	15
1951	8,133	6,813	1,320	16
1952	7,459	6,604	855	12
1953	7,928	7,079	849	11

SOURCE: Registrar, San Jose State College.

times abrupt shifts in absolute and relative size of the junior college operation do not appear to have been occasioned by changes in the qualifications and intentions of students, but related to problems of state college administration. The two low periods coincided with the student shortage of World War II and the time after 1948 when it was state policy to effect a separation of the junior college. In the latter period, the junior college shrank in numbers while the state college enrollment was at an all-time high. The junior college account clearly lent itself to flexible bookkeeping.

THE RELUCTANT SEPARATION

A study of higher education in California, published in 1948, recommended that San Jose Junior College be divorced from the state college. Concerned with division of function in a state system of higher education, the survey hit hard at the existing scheme:[11]

> An examination of the present activities of the state colleges indicates that they are in many instances operating in areas that properly belong to the junior college. . . . It is undesirable for the state colleges to continue functions which belong to the junior colleges; it is unreasonable to expect the State to provide facilities for students who can be accommodated in junior colleges. . . .
>
> Two of the colleges, Fresno and San Jose, are operating junior colleges under contract with the governing boards of the local school systems. . . . In Fresno the number of students is small; in San Jose Junior College it is approximately 1,500. While it is undoubtedly true that such an arrangement has in the past been beneficial to both parties, the time has arrived for a discontinuance of the arrangement. . . . Especially in San Jose, where the college plant is so overcrowded as to make it

[11] *Report of Survey*, pp. 22–23.

> necessary to schedule classes from 7:30 A.M. until 10:00 P.M., it may be well to insist that the city school system provide quarters and administrative management for the junior college. . . . In San Jose, where the city school system may not be able immediately to find quarters for 1,500 students, the arrangement should be discontinued as soon as housing facilities can be provided. This should be in from one to three years.

Before the end of the same year, the San Jose superintendent of schools had conferred with officials of the California State Department of Education "on the junior college problem," reporting later to his board of education that "the State Department of Education has adopted as policy the Report of a Survey of the Needs of California in Higher Education" and that there was no likelihood whatever of reversing the decision that San Jose Junior College be separated from San Jose State College.[12] The board had earlier obtained an opinion from its legal counsel that it would be obligated to continue the college upon termination of the contractual arrangement.[13] The state did not set a deadline for separation at this time, the recommendation that it be done within one to three years was not heeded, but from 1948 on, the state made it clear that separation would have to be accomplished. With state officials seeking assurance that "definite steps" would be taken, the San Jose school board announced in October, 1948:[14]

> It was agreed that the Board of Education should adopt a long range program looking toward the establishment of a separate junior college plant in San Jose. It was agreed, as a matter of policy, that such a junior college would be primarily terminal in its nature and that the emphasis in curriculum

[12] San Jose Unified School District, Minutes of the Board of Education, Oct. 28, 1948.

[13] *Ibid.*, July 1, 1948.

[14] *Ibid.*, Oct. 28, 1948.

> should be on vocational and trade training. It was agreed that, toward this end, the proposed new San Jose Technical High School should be located on a site which would be adequate for the expansion of the Technical High School into a technical or trade school, which could offer the junior college program.

The statement thus looked toward the creation of a new college but a college that would be linked with a technical high school.

This policy was implemented in part during the next five years by investment in land and building. A 50-acre site, considered suitable for "combined technical high school and junior college purposes," [15] was obtained. Then, "a trade training establishment, designed to accommodate students both on the high school and junior college level," [16] was constructed and equipped. This joint facility appealed financially to the school authorities because "it was felt enrollment on junior college level as well as high school level would justify the expenditure." [17] Further, this plant was seen as adaptable to future shifts in enrollment: "It was recognized . . . that this trade school might have a majority of high school students under one set of circumstances and, under other circumstances, the attendance might be made up almost exclusively of junior college students." [18] The Technical High School was moved to this joint site in the fall of 1952.

Because of the financial attractiveness of the arrangement with the state college, however, the San Jose schools remained reluctant to initiate a new college and finally did so only under increased pressure from the state. The decision to separate was

[15] San Jose Unified School District, Statement of Policy, Problems Attending the Reorganization of the San Jose Junior College, Jan. 22, 1953.

[16] *Ibid.*

[17] *Ibid.*

[18] San Jose Unified School District, Minutes of the Board of Education, Oct. 28, 1948.

prompted by an "ultimatum" from the state department of education, backed by the sanction of a "penalty charge." In the 1952–1953 contract between the district and the state college for the maintenance of the junior college operation, it was "expressly understood and agreed that the State does not contemplate the extension of the term hereof or the renewal of this contract." [19] The "contemplation" of the state department was backed with a plan to increase the annual bill to the San Jose schools by $100 per student, doubling the amount the district previously paid. With this, "the Board of Education, understandably, takes a much dimmer view than formerly of the financial attractiveness of having State College handle the district's junior college." [20] The district was clearly confronting a situation in which the state department of education had the means of ultimately bringing district policy in line with state policy.

With separation pending, the district appointed a study group on problems of separation in the fall of 1951. This committee prepared reports on three fields of education thought appropriate for the new college—business education, vocational and technical education, and general and terminal education—which were turned over to the first director of the college upon his appointment in November, 1952. The director, aided by a small part-time staff, continued planning throughout the rest of the 1952–1953 school year. The separate junior college opened for the 1953–1954 academic year on a campus shared with the Technical High School. In personnel, the college was a new organization. All administrators were new, and the only connection with the earlier operation consisted of four teachers who transferred from the state college.

[19] *Ibid.*, July 24, 1952.

[20] San Jose Unified School District, Statement of Policy, Problems Attending the Reorganization of the San Jose Junior College, Jan. 22, 1953.

THE DISTRICT POINT OF VIEW

Three types of district government are available for the administration of public junior colleges in California—the unified school district, the high school district, and the junior college district. Within the latter form, which contains no public schools other than the junior college, junior college personnel answer only to their own governing board. The board of a junior college district, conversely, need not concern itself with the managing of other types of schools. Moreover, if the district contains only one junior college, there is no central-headquarters staff interposed between operating personnel and controlling board. The director or president of the college is then the ranking educator, his position being analogous to that of superintendent in other districts. For more than one junior college in such a district, a central-headquarters staff is likely to be created, but such a staff will be concerned only with junior college problems. This autonomous form of control, which separates the junior college from the rest of local school government, is widely preferred by junior college administrators.

The other two forms of district organization generally permit less autonomy. Placed in a high school district, the junior college comes under a board of education with high school responsibilities; in a unified district, under a board responsible for the gamut of public school education. The jurisdiction of the unified district extends from kindergarten through grade 14; this is a form of school government calculated to promote vertical integration. It is also possible for one board to sit concurrently as the governing body for elementary, high school, and junior college districts that are legally separated. This system of government, found in the large Los Angeles school system, approaches the unified district in its possibilities for integrating school management.

The relative frequency of the three legal entities in California is indicated by the following: of fifty-three districts maintaining junior colleges in 1956–1957, twenty-three (43 per cent) were junior college districts, eighteen (34 per cent) were high school districts, and twelve (23 per cent) were unified districts.[21] The high school and unified districts, in which the administration of a junior college is closely linked with that of other schools, were thus more frequent (57 per cent) than separate junior college governments. In addition, nearly all major cities of the state that have junior colleges are under the unified plan. The twelve unified districts are: Fresno, Glendale, Long Beach, Oakland, Palos Verdes, Sacramento, San Diego, San Francisco, San Jose, Santa Monica, Stockton, and Vallejo. Thus the form of school government under which the new San Jose Junior College found itself is widely and importantly represented in the state, and the district frameworks that provide for integration with other levels of the public schools predominate in the state junior college system.

The San Jose Junior College is governed by a board of education and a district-headquarters staff which, in 1954–1955, was also responsible for twenty-two elementary schools, five junior high schools, five senior high schools, an adult education department, and related service units (see Chart 1). The school board of five members elected for three-year terms consisted of a businessman, an attorney, a union official, a college professor, and a housewife. The junior college relates to the board through a headquarters staff that consists of a superintendent of schools, a deputy superintendent, an assistant superintendent in charge of instruction, a business manager, and more than a dozen divisions grouped into three departments. For this central staff as well as for the board itself, the college is clearly only one of a host of concerns. The district was responsible for more than

[21] *Apportionment of the State School Fund, Part I, Year Ending June 30, 1957,* California State Department of Education, Sacramento, 1957, pp. 112–115.

Chart 1

Organization Structure of the San Jose Unified School District

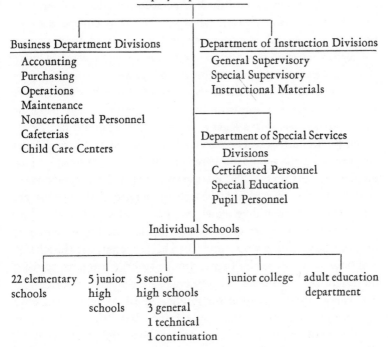

- Board of Education
  - Superintendent of Schools
    - Deputy Superintendent
      - Business Department Divisions
        - Accounting
        - Purchasing
        - Operations
        - Maintenance
        - Noncertificated Personnel
        - Cafeterias
        - Child Care Centers
      - Department of Instruction Divisions
        - General Supervisory
        - Special Supervisory
        - Instructional Materials
      - Department of Special Services Divisions
        - Certificated Personnel
        - Special Education
        - Pupil Personnel
      - Individual Schools
        - 22 elementary schools
        - 5 junior high schools
        - 5 senior high schools
          - 3 general
          - 1 technical
          - 1 continuation
        - junior college
        - adult education department

SOURCE: San Jose Unified School District, "Organization Chart," May 20, 1955.

twenty thousand students in 1954–1955 and had a rapidly growing elementary and high school population.

This authority structure delimited and directed the administration of the college in numerous ways, introducing district problems and a district point of view. District authorities, of course, are responsible for the welfare of an entire system. Their problems are those of central management—the general allocation of funds, the jurisdiction of subunits, the assignment of key administrative personnel, the maintenance of system-wide morale. It is to be expected that headquarters will have the balance of the whole as a natural concern and that headquarters and field units will have somewhat different perspectives. The top authorities of the San Jose district perceived the new college through the eyes of central management and transmitted to it certain concerns that were constricting from the college's point of view. Basic in district control was fiscal policy, and the financing of the college clearly exhibited the play of district concerns. For one, state college administration of the junior college program for three decades left a legacy in the city that could not be ignored by the district. The financial attractiveness of the former contractual arrangement lingered in San Jose as a model of junior college financing. The district was warned by a taxpayers' association the year before the college opened that costs of the separate college would be closely watched and compared to those of the past. In a report incorporated in the minutes of the board of education, this group said: "In the last analysis, the citizen will have to appraise the future Junior College program to see if increased costs balance with increased educational values." [22] The report then presented for public record an analysis of costs for the previous four years, specifying that "this information should prove useful for future reference and evaluation." [23] The question was raised anew at a late date whether nonrenewal of the previous contract with the state college was final; this

[22] "Let's Look at Local Government," *Report Submitted to the Board of Education by the Santa Clara County Taxpayers' Association,* San Jose Unified School District, Minutes of the Board of Education, Nov. 20, 1952.

[23] *Ibid.*

group claimed that a legal challenge of the separation could be made.[24] The concern of the district with this form of opposition to the new college was soon in evidence:[25]

> The Board of Education further believes there is misapprehension on the part of many respecting the cost of the junior college program the district plans to conduct, as compared to costs when the services were contracted to San Jose State College. . . . Actually, the operating costs will be little if any more than they would be if the contract with state college, carrying the new $100 per student charge, were renewed.

Thus, an important lay group was using the former arrangement as its frame of reference and, willingly or not, the school authorities were also using preseparation costs as a base line.

The support of the college from local tax funds was therefore kept at a low point, near that established as the norm in the early period, with the college financed largely from outside sources. In the college's fourth year, revenue was approximately 170 per cent of costs, with income from outside sources alone equal to 95 per cent of operating expenditures. (For absolute figures see Table 2.) Locally derived income hardly needed to be touched, although normally in California local revenue assumes one-half to two-thirds of the burden of school expenditures. The district set aside some money from current income for capital outlay on new junior college buildings, and after this still had a surplus of about $400,000 per year. As seen in Table 2, this was comparable with the annual surplus of the preseparation years. This meant that the college was not receiving the revenue raised by the district's junior college tax. From the standpoint of the college, the district was continuing to treat the junior

[24] *Ibid.*

[25] San Jose Unified School District, Statement of Policy, Problems Attending the Reorganization of the San Jose Junior College, Jan. 22, 1953.

Table 2

Revenue and Cost of San Jose Junior College, 1950–1951 to 1956–1957

	Preseparation years			First four years of separate organization			
	1950–1951	1951–1952	1952–1953	1953–1954	1954–1955	1955–1956	1956–1957
Average daily attendance (ADA)	1,135	732	628	1,036	2,158	2,498	2,872
Operating costs:							
Amount	$385,937	$375,210	$397,369	$319,710	$530,190	$ 732,127	$ 950,921
Per ADA	340	513	633	309	246	293	331
Revenue:*							
State aid	$ 96,410	$104,150	$ 67,880	$139,263	$253,892	$ 316,034	$ 420,935
Tuition from other districts	201,587	248,942	214,794	282,375	159,931	330,975	482,287
Local junior college tax	420,266	464,371	514,333	532,377	572,323	593,623	698,967
Total revenue	$718,263	$817,463	$797,007	$954,015	$986,146	$1,240,632	$1,602,189
Excess of revenue over costs	$332,326	$442,253	$399,638	$634,305	$455,956	$ 508,505	$ 651,268
Revenue committed to capital outlay†	None	None	None	210,231	77,532	77,641	232,019
Surplus	332,326	442,253	399,638	424,074	378,424	430,864	419,249

* Federal funds excluded because data not available. If included, total revenue would have been about 3 to 5 per cent higher for most of the above years.

† Capital outlay normally comes from school-bond income rather than from current operating revenue. The district used $1,232,848 for capital outlay on the junior college from bond income during 1954–1955 and 1955–1956 in addition to the money reported above.

SOURCE: San Jose Unified School District records.

college operation as a money-maker, its tax yield being used by other schools.

The central authorities of the district took a jaundiced view of college personnel reasoning along these lines, because the district officials were mindful of the possibilities of effective district management. The outlook of district headquarters was summed up in the phrase "We are a unified school district." This means in fiscal policy that all income is *district* income and that in practice there is no such thing as "junior college income." For example, the district is reluctant to break down the local tax rate into elementary, high school, and junior college components, preferring to think in terms of one total district rate. Budgets of the district show just a single total tax-rate figure, and returns from this tax are reported as one lump sum under "non-earmarked" current revenues.[26] From the district's point of view, there is no need to budget one program or level of education in proportion to its part in producing revenue. Since requirements of the various schools change through time, the district would like to be free to distribute funds internally at its own discretion. Earmarked funds clearly reduce flexibility. "We are a unified school district" also means that the system as a whole has commitments and problems that the component schools cannot reasonably expect to ignore. The district faced not only the tradition of an inexpensive junior college operation but also major expansion for a rapidly growing elementary school population.

For the new college, however, its level of financing was clearly a heavy burden. The financial restraint produced in this case by a unified-district position hit home with college personnel when they made the inevitable comparison between what they were receiving from the district and what they would automatically receive in a more independent position, that is, the full return from junior college revenues. The first director of the college

[26] San Jose Unified School District, *Budgets for 1953–1954, 1954–1955, 1955–1956, 1956–1957.*

maintained at the end of two years of work that the existing state of affairs was one entailing "the lowest junior college instructional cost per unit of ADA [average daily attendance] we have ever seen reported anywhere, for any Junior College in California." [27] The director compared his own unit expenditure ($309 in 1953–1954) with that of several other junior colleges, ranging from $435 to $625, and suggested that the California average was near $500. He also made a comparison with the high schools of the district whose unit cost that year was $468 or approximately 50 per cent higher than that of the college.[28] The expense figure for the college was considerably below that set in the state's foundation program for junior college education ($380), which the state considers a minimum acceptable level of support. An index of district support is presented in Table 3, comparing San Jose's expenditure for three levels of education with the state's idea of acceptable minimums. As can be seen, the state expects junior colleges to be more expensive than high schools and elementary schools. In San Jose these other schools are comparatively well financed while the junior college is supported at a level below that which the state believes is minimally acceptable.

The district point of view on supporting a separate college was not shaped by the expectations of lay groups alone. Some school personnel of the district similarly believed in restricting the college. The separate college naturally constituted one more competitor for school funds and was perceived as taking funds that otherwise would go into the payroll of the other schools and would be used for such purposes as the elimination of double sessions in the elementary schools. A conflict of interest, normal among units of a complex organization, was deepened by the

[27] *Report to Board of Education,* San Jose Unified School District, Mar. 17 and Mar. 18, 1955.

[28] *Ibid.*

Table 3

District Support of School Levels,
San Jose Unified School District,
1955–1956

Education level	Instructional unit cost,* dollars		Ratio of outlay to foundation program
	State foundation program†	San Jose outlay	
Elementary school	212	291	1.37
High school	280	531	1.90
Junior college	380	293	0.77

* Cost per unit of average daily attendance.

† A foundation program is intended to be a minimum acceptable level of school support.

SOURCES: State of California Education Code, Sacramento, 1955, secs. 7036, 7037.2, 7038; and *Statistical Data, 1956–57*, San Jose Unified School District, Mar. 1, 1957.

expectation, inherited from the past and built into the budget, that the junior college account should contribute funds for other uses. District tradition in this way contributed to a situation where in the district organization as a whole it was thought that the college would harm many persons and interests. This was a bread-and-butter concern, one of money rather than of doctrine, and although the separate college did not become a financial burden, personnel of the other schools continued to believe it did. "That white elephant called the Junior College," a "pet project" of the administration, was seen as a cause of "no money for teachers' raises." [29]

[29] *San Jose Mercury*, June 29, 1956.

Opposition to the college from the ranks of school personnel can be illustrated by considering the position held by one small but important group of opposing teachers. The San Jose unit (Local 957) of the American Federation of Teachers (AFT) had a number of reasons for opposing the college. One was the financial consideration discussed above. An AFT leader explained in an interview that it would have been cheaper for the district if the junior college had remained with the state college, even paying the $100-per-ADA fine levied by the state. The teachers of the district would then have had more money available for salaries. Secondly, the separate junior college was perceived as a project fostered by the administration. It was explained that the "district bosses" had not gone to the public with a bond issue to establish the separate college, but rather had built its initial physical plant from current school monies, "without much notice to anyone," and in conjunction with moving the San Jose Technical High School. It was maintained that the question of separation was not actually taken to the public but was treated as an administrative matter. A dislike of the administration's general style of operation was evident here.

A third basis for opposition from this teacher group was related to its status as part of the trade union movement. An interest in a terminal institution within the public schools, one that would have a vocational cast, stemmed from an organized labor view that there should be a type of school which prepares for skilled and semiskilled occupations. "The junior college could become this but rarely does," maintained an AFT respondent. The AFT was depicted as in favor of the junior college as an idea, but as not happy about the way junior colleges work out in practice. It was argued that the junior college is "sold" to the public in California as a terminal institution but that it always becomes a college transfer station. In San Jose, "the administration should have steered the junior college down the terminal road" from the beginning, guiding the students in such a way that the college would be at least two-thirds terminal. When the college did not become a vocational school,[30] the AFT was left holding on to the Technical High School as the only public school in San Jose that could be depended upon to maintain a blue-collar orientation. As will be seen in the following section, the AFT position was important because it linked teacher opposition with resistance to the new college that came from a specific quarter.

With such interests, contrary to a separate college, alive within the district and pushing in the same direction as outside economy-minded groups, the district-headquarters staff had considerable incentive to move slowly in supporting the college. Fiscal restraint was indicative of a general conservative outlook toward the district's newest branch. This attitude stemmed from the web of interests found in and around the school system and from the needs of unified-district management. The following section further elaborates this point, taking up the schools in the district that were most directly affected by the new college.

ORGANIZATIONAL DISPLACEMENT

Among other tasks, a comprehensive junior college may assume prime responsibility for vocational education in the schools. To do so, however, means that vocational programs under high school administration need to be redefined. Usually, general industrial arts programs are instituted in the regular comprehensive high school, and specialized vocational training is moved up to the junior college. This organization of programs, however, leaves little room for the special technical high school. When a new junior college enters a system which already contains a technical school, some organizational displacement is likely to

[30] See Chap. 2.

occur. This happened in San Jose when the rise of the college was related to the decline of the local technical school.

For some years before the 1953 separation of the college, the San Jose Technical High School had suffered the stigma frequently attached to vocational education generally and to public trade schools in particular. Leading directly to manual occupations, perceived as a "work" school, attended by male students of primarily low academic ability, its appeal to students had lessened at the same time that the comprehensive high school, with its elaborate complex of courses and activities, had become more attractive. To attend Tech High in San Jose meant to separate from friends who proceeded from the ninth grade of junior high school to the "regular" high schools and to bear the status of attending a "school for dummies." Students resisted going to such a school and, as enrollment remained low, a cycle of declining attractiveness set in. The school was forced to withdraw from an athletic league in 1952 because it could not field a football team. Technical High was one-fifth to one-fourth of the size of the regular high schools; for example, in 1955–1956 it had about 250 students compared to about 1,000 in each of three comprehensive high schools. The entering class in 1955 was 103, the smallest in more than twenty years except the year 1950.

Falling enrollment and a high drop-out rate in an expensive physical plant rendered the school a costly operation for the district, with unit cost (more than $600) higher than in the other high schools and about double that of the new college. Decline was occurring at the same time that the San Jose metropolitan area was undergoing considerable population expansion and the rest of the school system was growing rapidly.[31] There were

[31] The population of the city of San Jose increased 33.9 per cent between 1950 and 1956, from 95,280 to 127,564; and the San Jose metropolitan area (Santa Clara County) in the same period, from 288,292 to 461,700 (estimated) or 60.2 per cent. The expansion of the San Jose school population for these six years was from 15,600 units of average daily attendance in 1950–

compelling reasons for the school authorities to regard Tech High as a "sick child" and to want to eliminate it. Educational doctrine also encouraged discontinuance, because California educators have favored comprehensive high schools and the elimination of the specialized school. The tendency in the state, as suggested previously, has been to divide the vocational work of the public schools between the comprehensive high school and the junior college.

Revision and relocation of vocational training had been in the minds of district authorities since at least 1948, when the board of education issued its first policy statement on the separation of the junior college.[32] That document proposed a "trade training establishment" jointly occupied by Technical High and the junior college, and suggested that this center might have largely high school students at one time or "almost exclusively" junior college students at another. If it was not clear in 1948 which of these two possibilities was more likely, it was apparent after 1953. Tech High remained small, while the junior college grew rapidly and came to dominate the combined campus. Enrollment, buildings, and staff accrued to the college. With this trend, a recommendation was made by the superintendent of schools to the board of education in January, 1955, to close the technical school.[33] Under his proposed plan, the school would continue only until its current students graduated, with a "gradual transition of the program to the Junior College level." The school would

1951 to 21,827 in 1955–1956, or 39.9 per cent. U.S. Bureau of the Census, "Special Census of San Jose, California, Oct. 4, 1956," in *Current Population Reports, Special Censuses*, ser. P-28, no. 968, Mar. 11, 1957, p. 1; *California's Population in 1956*, California Department of Finance, Sacramento, July, 1956, p. 13; and San Jose Unified School District, *Budget, 1956–1957*, August, 1956, p. 11.

[32] See pp. 16–17.

[33] "Report on Reorganization of Trade and Industrial Education," letter to the Board of Education from the superintendent of schools, San Jose Unified School District, Minutes of the Board of Education, Jan. 20, 1955.

terminate at the end of the 1956–1957 school year, the junior college then taking over the campus.

The matter was not to be this simple, however, for the technical school resisted burial. Its staff was reluctant to accept its demise and it had support in the city. The building trades of the area had received many students from the school over the years, and members of the building trade unions taught such subjects as carpentry, painting, plumbing, and electrical work in the school. The school had allies in both the firms for which personnel were trained and in the trade unions for which it was a source of apprentices and a symbol of a distinctive place for vocational training. From the ranks of these friends a technical school bloc was organized immediately after the recommendation of the superintendent had been submitted to the school board. Their purpose was "to save Tech High." From the outset these supporters were hostile to the junior college because it figured centrally in district policy as an alternative to Technical High.

Various organizations connected with this group waged a campaign throughout 1955 and 1956 in the press, on the speaker's platform and at board of education meetings. At the first two board meetings following the superintendent's report, the school board heard in person or in writing from the Santa Clara County Apprenticeship Advisory Committee, the Building and Construction Trades Council, the Technical High Faculty Club, and technical school students.[34] At later meetings it heard from many other labor bodies such as the Central Labor Council of Santa Clara County, the Allied Printing Trades Council of San Jose, and the Sheet Metal Workers International Association,[35] all arguing for continuing and strengthening the separate technical school. The technical school supporters were able to rally

[34] San Jose Unified School District, Minutes of the Board of Education, Feb. 3 and Feb. 17, 1955.

[35] *Ibid.*, Jan. 19, 1956.

more than fifty organizations for their cause, including the San Jose local of the American Federation of Teachers.[36] In arguing for the technical school, the leaders of this bloc presented an image of the junior college as ill-conceived in policy and poorly executed in practice. The college was depicted as a "promotion scheme of certain professional educators, and also, the Department of Education of California." [37] As a scheme, it was designed to kill off the technical school. Yet, this group maintained, the college could not adequately replace the technical school because in the college vocational education would be subordinate to academic interests. The college's primary interest in college transfer programs was said to mean, too, that "the prime purpose and original intent of this institution is not being filled." [38] At the same time, however, the college was not much of a college at that, since it was a home for "State College culls." [39] Operationally, the college "overshadowed" the school on the jointly occupied campus, increasingly "encroaching" on the technical school facilities. The attitude of the first director of the college was "one of resentment, intolerance, inconsideration, and at times scornfulness with respect to the Technical High School." [40] These conceptions, frequently and militantly presented, received support within the school system from teachers of other than technical subjects. Teachers for whom the college was suspect because of its apparent impingement on their own interests sympathized with the tenor of much of the criticism. The AFT local was the most active group among the teachers, its leadership par-

[36] *Report (of the Minority) of the Study Committee for Industrial Education,* San Jose Unified School District, March, 1956, pp. 34–35.

[37] *Ibid.,* p. 20.

[38] *Ibid.,* p. 18.

[39] Board of Education Special Session, Apr. 23, 1956; author's field notes.

[40] *Report (of the Minority) of the Study Committee for Industrial Education,* San Jose Unified School District, March, 1956, p. 11.

ticipating in the committees organized by this faction. In its open opposition it was joined by the state office of the American Federation of Teachers which, in a published letter, argued that the "educational fakirs" of the state had been planning for some time "the emasculation of the Vocational shop program," turning work at the high school level into a "toy factory" and benefiting only the junior college.[41]

No support for the college was forthcoming from any teacher or administrative groups during this time, and little defense of the college was made by the district while this public campaign was under way. College spokesmen themselves were restrained by district headquarters from publicly answering the criticism, leaving the college on the defensive in its relationships with the community. The district attempted to counter the pressure exerted upon it by appointing a study committee for industrial education, with representatives from the state department of education, local firms and unions, and the district. Asked to bring in recommendations on the handling of technical and industrial education throughout the San Jose school system, the committee itself soon became deeply divided, with a technical high school minority at odds with the majority. Two reports were brought in to the school board in March, 1956, one for the district and one vigorously for the separate vocational school. The work of the committee clearly failed to resolve the controversy, and the district fell back on a plan whereby high school students who wanted vocational work could attend a regular high school and be transported to the technical school facilities for part-time training.[42] In line with the recommendation of the committee majority, the district supported the initial recommendation of the superintendent to close out full-time students at

[41] Letter to Santa Clara County Education League from California State Federation of Teachers, Apr. 3, 1956, *ibid.*, p. 39.

[42] San Jose Unified School District, Minutes of the Board of Education, May 3, 1956.

the technical school. At the same time, the existence of students there on a part-time basis kept alive the technical school use of the jointly occupied campus. The school board also created a position of director of vocational education within the administrative structure of district headquarters.[43] These changes were followed a year later by board policies that "the facilities of the Technical High School will continue to be the service unit for vocational-industrial education for high school students and . . . shall be known as the Vocational Center"; further, "high school students will have first priority in the use of the vocational center facilities," and "when high school student requests have been filled, junior college students, on approval of the Director of Vocational Education, may be enrolled in vocational classes offered at the Vocational Center."[44] In this way the technical school was "saved" and the vocational education part of the junior college placed under the supervision of a headquarters director. As an upshot of the technical school controversy, the authority of the college in operating its own programs was made more limited than before. The expanded authority of the new vocational education director could also be taken as an indication of a district point of view on integration and central control. An additional administrative link was forged between the college and district headquarters.

Adult Education

Another area of work in which a new public junior college is likely to overlap with the interests of other schools is adult education.[45] In the junior college, adult education is frequently

[43] *Ibid.*

[44] *Ibid.*, June 6, 1957.

[45] See Burton R. Clark, *Adult Education in Transition: A Study of Institutional Insecurity*, University of California Press, Berkeley, Calif., 1956, pp. 130–141.

found under the rubrics of "extended day" or "junior college education for part-time students." Whatever the name, classes for adults are made available that compete with adult schools in jurisdiction and clientele. An adult education program of some reputation had existed in San Jose long before the opening of the college, under the administration of a department of adult education. This department had half a dozen centers, chiefly located in high school buildings. It also contained a legal entity called the San Jose Evening Junior College, for the purpose of granting course credit to students who wanted to work toward a junior college degree (associate in arts). The department prided itself on discussion courses in the liberal arts and social-civic affairs, and also provided the usual array of adult education courses in arts and crafts, Americanization, family living, and business and vocational subjects. The department's jurisdiction in clientele, courses, and physical facilities encompassed the education of the adult in the San Jose district.

With the advent of the college, this jurisdiction became partly unhinged, because the college soon developed an evening program open to adults. A major unit of the department of adult education, the San Jose Vocational Evening High School, was removed from its jurisdiction and reconstituted as part of the college.[46] The department became quickly interested in keeping adult education out of the college, and was largely able to do so in other than vocational education. The college found that the district continued to give primary responsibility to the department in adult education, and it was restrained from developing a program of nonvocational offerings. As will be seen in Chapter 3, the evening work of the college remained overwhelmingly vocational.

By this restriction the impact of precedence and prerogative within a parent system was demonstrated. The college was not in an independent position where it could develop its programs

[46] See Chap. 3.

for part-time students as it saw fit. What it wanted to do had to be considered by the district officials in the light of the traditional rights of the established department and the influence of that department in and outside the district. The college was hardly in a position to assert itself vigorously in this direction, for it faced more fundamental problems in finance, rapid growth, and the technical school controversy. The administrative placement of the college made it a direct threat to local adult schools, posing the possibility of displacing or redefining their work. The resistance that was called out stemmed from overlapping interests within a larger administrative system.

THE STATE COLLEGE

Outside the district, San Jose State College was the single organization that had an extensive impact on the new junior college. The state college's administration of a junior college program before 1953, as earlier explained, caused certain expectations to arise in San Jose that were later difficult to shed. In addition, the state college preempted local support for higher education. One reason why a new junior college is often welcomed in a city is that it gives the home town a college, a local unit of higher education from which stems prestige and financial gain. Community identification on such bases was not readily available for the new San Jose Junior College, because local loyalties had long been centered on San Jose State. As the oldest public college in California, it had become a local "institution" by age alone. It had also touched several generations of local business and political leaders and could draw upon their loyalty as alumni. When, in 1955, the state college was in difficulty with the state over limitations on size, the mayor of the city of San Jose spoke in its behalf:[47]

[47] *Twelfth Report, Senate Investigating Committee on Education,* California State Senate, S. Res. 168 (1953), 1955, p. 23.

> Inasmuch as most of our grandparents, our parents, ourselves, and our children have attended San Jose State College, we are deeply interested in the problem at present that exists at the college. It is a major concern to all that we can hardly take care of the people who live in the immediate service area . . . and that we must do everything we can to rectify this grave condition.

The mayor's use of "we" in referring to the San Jose State College was seconded by the manager of the San Jose Chamber of Commerce, who referred to the college as "our state college."[48] No similar statements of support for the junior college were ever forthcoming from local political and business leaders. The state college also had considerable economic value locally, through its own expenditures and that of students in residence. In addition, as a baccalaureate college that also had some programs leading to a master's degree, it had a degree-granting status that could not be approached by the junior college. The existence of the state college in San Jose, not more than three miles from the new junior college, meant both a preemption of and a higher call upon community pride.

The impact of the state college was also felt through students. As will be seen in Chapter 2, most junior college students who want a bachelor's degree have the San Jose State College in mind as the college to which they will transfer. These students would begin their college education at the state college and remain there, if they could. Many initiate study at the junior college after unsuccessful attendance at the senior college. This means that the admission and retention practices of the San Jose State College affect the number and kind of students the junior college will receive. If the state college lowers its entrance requirements or fails few students, it can immediately draw students from the junior college; if it raises its standards of admission or fails large

[48] *Ibid.*, p. 24.

numbers, it can flood the junior college with students. The presence of a college of higher status nearby sharply affects the degree of control the junior college has over the size, composition, and duration of its own student body. The stability of the junior college is partly dependent on state college decision-making, which is done independently of local school authorities.

A CONCLUSION

This chapter has concentrated on certain features of the immediate environment of a new junior college as they were organized by the administrative system of which the college was made a part. The larger system had certain general consequences for the college. Basic was the fact that public school authorities set the terms of existence. Empirical evidence of this was apparent in the financing of the college. Managed as an integral part of the public schools, the college was brought in line with needs of the central district management. From the point of view of the college, district control was heavily constraining.

A second general consequence—that public school "interest groups" affected the development of the college—is closely related to the first. These groups were both internal and external to the district. Among them were the staff of the Technical High School, a bloc of community supporters of the technical school, the adult education department, and elementary and high school personnel generally. As an integral part of the public schools, the junior college also found itself related to the needs of other component schools of the district. Directly affected by these needs was the college's authority over its own vocational program and its jurisdiction in adult education. More indirectly, the college's external affairs began on poor footing.

In short, the college's administrative location meant that the controls, orientations, and pressures of public school administration would inescapably shape its character.

The over-all value of integrated school management depends on many effects other than the one considered here, and no general conclusion about the unified district should be drawn on this one ground alone. The worth of the Technical High School and the adult school was similarly not at issue here, nor were other administrative systems in which junior colleges may be placed examined or recommended over the one at hand. The analysis was limited to the impact of one type of administrative setting on the development of a new college.

CHAPTER 2

The Open Door

A second major determinant of the character of a college is the kind of student body it is able to attract. Students affect a college in many ways, from the quality of participation and performance in the individual classroom to the general image of the college held by the public. Their characteristics set many of the terms under which organizational work is done. This is so well understood in most colleges that a key question asked by faculty and administration is, Who shall be admitted? A considerable burden is thrown on admission policies, because they are expected to shape the student base that in turn will shape the college. This cycle of effects raises a number of questions discussed in this chapter: What is the admission policy of the college and how was it determined? What kind of student body is produced, in terms of what the students want to do, their ability, and their background? What is the length of stay and academic destiny of the students? What are the character-shaping consequences of admission policy and student characteristics? The final section of the chapter identifies a distinctive task set for the college by the nature of its student body and suggests ways in which the work of the college is thereby shaped.

This task, as well as other effects described in Chapter 3, are linked to what may be called the open-door policy of admissions. Public junior colleges generally have a similar policy and a similar kind of student body on most characteristics highlighted here, despite somewhat different administrative frameworks. The "open door" is a primary attribute of the American junior college, especially the locally controlled version.

THE DISTRICT VERSUS THE STUDENT

A source of strain and confusion in the development of the junior college in San Jose lay in the conflict between the intentions of the district fathers and the wishes of the college's students. The San Jose school authorities wanted the college to emphasize terminal vocational education. The 1948 statement of policy of the San Jose Board of Education, reviewed in the previous chapter, stated that the "junior college would be primarily terminal in its nature and the emphasis in curriculum should be on vocational and trade training." It further said: "Toward this end, the proposed new San Jose Technical High School should be located on a site which would be adequate for the expansion of the Technical High School into a technical or trade school, which could offer the junior college program." [1] This vocational policy became expressed in the physical plant of the college, with the major structures of the initial campus limited to the vocational shops of this joint "trade training establishment." The initial administrative structure and administrative personnel of the college also reflected a vocational outlook.

This trade school image came from many sources. Foremost was the hope of the district that, as a vocational center, the college would help solve the Technical High School problem and would provide vocational training after high school. There was also some interest in building a school that would not extensively

[1] San Jose Unified School District, Minutes of the Board of Education, Oct. 28, 1948.

overlap the work of the nearby state college. The district superintendent stated in 1952 that "the problem which confronts the city schools is to develop an institution which will not duplicate the offerings of San Jose State College, but which will still meet the needs of the young people of the Community." [2] Transfer programs would be duplicating for the most part, while two-year technical curricula would be remote from the work of a four-year college. A terminal emphasis would also give the college a claim to uniqueness, since no other school or college in the San Jose metropolitan area had a college-level program of this type. With this, the district would be squarely in line with junior college doctrine. National spokesmen for the junior college strongly accentuate the value of the two-year terminal work and portray it as the special contribution of the junior college. As one group put it:[3]

> The four-year college and the university can certainly provide a major part of the needed additional facilities for education beyond high school. . . . But these institutions best serve the requirements of students who seek four or more years of higher education. . . . Programs of less than four years are best furnished by a different type of institution—a college where the attention of faculty, administration, and board of control will be directed particularly to the needs and goals of students whose formal education is limited to one or two years beyond high school. The junior college is uniquely adapted to these ends.

This emphasis in San Jose was apparently never intended as a sole commitment, however, and leeway was allowed in the new college for other activities. The junior college had pretransfer

[2] San Jose Unified School District, Meeting of Representatives to Consider Problems Associated with Separating San Jose Junior College from San Jose State College, Oct. 3, 1952.

[3] National Society for the Study of Education, Yearbook Committee, "The Role of the Public Junior College," *The Public Junior College,* Fifty-fifth Yearbook, University of Chicago Press, Chicago, 1956, part 1, p. 66.

students during the time it was a part of state college administration, and there was no compelling reason upon separation to forego this work. The junior college movement, while interested in the terminal operation as a special feature, believes in multipurpose schools. In California nearly all junior colleges are of a comprehensive type; multiple responsibilities for the junior college are part of the philosophy of the state system and are described in the state education code:[4]

> The course of study for two-year junior colleges shall be designed to fit the needs of pupils of the thirteenth and fourteenth grades and may include courses of instruction designed to prepare for admission to the upper division of higher institutions of learning and such other courses of instruction designed to prepare persons for agricultural, commercial, homemaking, industrial and other vocations, and such courses of instruction as may be deemed necessary to provide for the civic and liberal education of the citizens of the community.

This sets forth the purposes of (1) lower-division pretransfer education, (2) vocational and technical education of a terminal sort, and (3) adult education. These state provisions are permissive rather than mandatory for the individual junior college, but they reflect and contribute to the expectation that the junior college will be a comprehensive school.

Central to the conception of the junior college as a comprehensive school is state policy on junior college admissions. As expressed in the education code: "The principal of any two-year junior college shall admit to the junior college any high school graduate and any other person over 18 years of age who in his judgment is capable of profiting from the instruction offered."[5]

[4] State of California Education Code, Sacramento, 1955, sec. 10602.

[5] *Ibid.*, sec. 8821. This admission policy is not unique to California but rather is the most common policy for the public junior college throughout the country. See Leland L. Medsker, *The Junior College: Progress and Prospect*, McGraw-Hill Book Company, Inc., New York, 1960, chap. 8.

This principle is construed by school administrators in the state to mean that the junior college should not attempt to select; further, "those responsible for the junior colleges are opposed to any selection of students through admission procedures."[6] The "shall admit" provision in the code statement is regarded by junior college administrators as a mandate that places the burden of proof on the official who would reject a student. A case would need to be made, it is argued, that the prospective student could not profit from any work of the junior college. This constitutes an effective block to any tendency to select. In effect, the junior college is expected to admit all applicants, without regard to ability, type of curriculum completed in high school, or any other aspect of background. It is to have an open door.

The open-door outlook is generally extended in junior colleges to the belief that the incoming student should also have unrestricted choice in electing a field of study. This includes the basic alternative of whether to enter into a transfer or a terminal curriculum. San Jose Junior College offered transfer work from the start and the college's administrators did not feel they had the authority to deny access to it, regardless of the college potential of the student. An unfettered choice of program became a part of the open-door policy. For San Jose and the state as a whole, these student prerogatives mean that the public junior college has nonselected student bodies, the individual student being entitled to an unrestricted choice of programs within the wide limits of a comprehensive school. In effect the student constituency of a junior college is entitled to determine what the college will emphasize.

It thus mattered little what purposes the San Jose school authorities wanted to emphasize, because under these terms of existence the preferences of self-selected students would basically orient the college. The preference of San Jose students was to en-

[6] *Restudy*, p. 114.

ter the programs that lead toward a bachelor's degree. Throughout the college's early years the students chose transfer majors. Sixty per cent of the students in the first semester of the college enrolled in curricula leading to a bachelor's degree (see Table 4). The transfer segment of total enrollment increased in each of the three succeeding years, exceeding 75 per cent in the third and fourth years. This level compares with that commonly found in junior colleges throughout the country; transfer enrollment will amount to two-thirds to three-fourths of total enrollment.[7] This percentage increase represented a large increase in absolute numbers, for the college was growing rapidly throughout this period. Enrollment increased more than 150 per cent between the first and second years, and nearly 300 per cent between the first and fourth years. The number of transfer-minded students increased fivefold, and amounted to more than sixteen hundred full-time students at the beginning of the fourth year. The number of terminal students, meanwhile, increased about 2½ times, from approximately two hundred to five hundred.

The build-up of the transfer operation was concretely experienced by the personnel of the college. As district headquarters held to its original statement of purpose, the divergence between what was occurring and what was supposed to be happening strained relations between the college and the central district staff. The first director of the college, who was on the scene for the first two years, maintained vigorously that the predominance of the transfer operation had to be recognized as a fact of life. In a major report to the board of education, the director, near the end of his stay in office, reviewed the change that had occurred in the following terms:[8]

[7] See Medsker, *op. cit.*, chap. 4.

[8] "San Jose Junior College," *Report to Board of Education*, San Jose Unified School District, Mar. 17 and Mar. 18, 1955, part 4, pp. 1–2.

Table 4
Transfer and Terminal Students* of San Jose Junior College, 1953–1954 to 1956–1957

Year and semester	Transfer enrollment		Terminal enrollment		Total enrollment		Increase over first year	
	Number	Per cent	Number	Per cent	Number	Per cent	Number	Per cent
First year (1953–1954):								
Fall	321	60	218	40	539	100		
Spring	354	57	271	43	625	100		
Second year (1954–1955):								
Fall	901	66	475	34	1,376	100	837	155
Spring	1,053	69	470	31	1,523	100		
Third year (1955–1956):								
Fall	1,359	76	429	24	1,788	100	1,249	232
Spring	1,370	76	430	24	1,800	100		
Fourth year (1956–1957):								
Fall	1,631	76	502	24	2,133	100	1,594	296
Spring	1,381	75	466	25	1,847	100		

* Enrollment of full-time day students at the beginning of each semester.

SOURCE: San Jose Junior College, Division of Student Services.

> The original concept of San Jose Junior College as a vocational-technical institution with an enrollment of some 750 students by 1955–56, has already been more than fulfilled by 1954–55. However, a situation which was not foreseen in the Fall of 1952, and which began to become apparent by February of 1953, is that the vocational-technical program which we are now offering—even though larger than our original estimates—has been far outstripped by the four-year college transfer programs, although originally these were erroneously believed to be only a minor part of our total operation.

The director stressed the fact that an enormous overload of work had occurred, especially in the first year, "because we were compelled on our opening date to put a complete lower division college program into immediate operation." [9] By the end of the second year, the college had "approximately thirty reasonably well-organized curricula in the general education and lower division fields." [10] The director concluded that "the uncertainties of opinion and conjecture, which surrounded our organizational period, have been replaced by the facts of on-the-job experience. It is time for a reevaluation of our current status and future prospect in the light of these facts." [11]

The college thus did not actually become an upgraded technical high school, and it was not to accentuate terminal curricula. The stated purpose of the district went relatively unimplemented, while other ends took over that were originally defined as minor by the school authorities. These were set by students interested in pursuing an extended college education. Their desires determined that the college was to become a place where unselected students engage in a college "tryout." The power to determine objectives was actually widely diffused rather than concentrated in the hands of a central staff of educators.

[9] *Ibid.*, p. 2.
[10] *Ibid.*, p. 4.
[11] *Ibid.*, part 1, p. 1.

STUDENT ABILITY

The students of the college, then, were unselected and transfer-oriented. What of their ability? Here again the college found its student body shaped by the place of the junior college within the structure of California higher education. In the state's three-segment system—university, state college, and junior college—the state university has a student body relatively high in academic ability, the state college has students that in the aggregate are of lesser ability, and the junior college has the lowest average of the three. These ability differences follow from a differentiation of functions and different degrees of selectivity in entrance requirements. A general picture of this academic differentiation was shown in a 1955 state study.[12] On aptitude examinations[13] given to freshman entrants in 1952 or 1953, the university "exceeded by a wide margin" the average scores of students in the state colleges and junior colleges; from the other end, "the student bodies as a whole in the junior colleges were generally less able in terms of general scholastic aptitude than students in the state colleges and the university." [14] Comparisons were made by plotting medians and quartile scores against a scale derived from a nation-wide norm population. The median score for the university students was at the 73rd percentile on the national scale and hence considerably above the national average. Test data were available on nine state colleges and their medians ranged between 60 and 35 on the national scale. Four of the state colleges had medians over the national average (60, 60, 59, 51); five were

[12] *Restudy*, pp. 104–107.

[13] *The American Council Psychological Examination* (*College Edition*) was used in the state colleges and junior colleges. *The College Entrance Examination Board Scholastic Aptitude Test* was used in the University of California and approximations of its results made to the norms for *The American Council Psychological Examination. Ibid.*

[14] *Ibid.*, pp. 104, 106.

below the national median; three between 40 and 50 (48, 46, 40); and two under 40 (35, 35). San Jose State College was near the middle of the state college range and near the national norm.

Of the twenty-eight public junior colleges reporting test data in the 1955 study, all were below the national norm and the median of the twenty-eight medians was 34. Four of the junior colleges had medians between 40 and 49 (49, 44, 40, 40); seventeen were between 30 and 39 (six at 35 or above and eleven below 35); six were spread through the 20-to-30 range; and one junior college had a median of 13. San Jose Junior College, which was still a part of the state college at the time these data were reported, was near the bottom of the junior college range.

Test data available from the college itself [15] indicate that as a separate organization its student body occupied about the same relative position as indicated above. Near the end of its second year (spring semester, 1954–1955), the college tested 1,011 students, 64 per cent of its day enrollment, on the American Council Psychological Examination and found that the median aptitude score was at the 29th percentile of the national scale. Students enrolled in transfer programs had a median score of 36; terminal students had a median score of 11 for those in a technical and industrial program and 13 for other two-year students. Test results at the end of the third year (spring semester, 1955–1956) showed that the college's aptitude median had fallen to 23. At that time, 7 per cent of the students scored above the 80th percentile of the national scale; at the other extreme of aptitude, 42 per cent scored below the 20th percentile. These data point to two conclusions: the range of ability among the students was great, and the student body as a whole had low college aptitude.

[15] San Jose Junior College, Division of Student Services, "San Jose Junior College," (mimeographed report on enrollment and student characteristics), Sept. 21, 1956.

Turning from aptitude to achievement, the college gave Stanford achievement tests in English and mathematics to 450 applicants for the fall of 1955. The test results were converted to grade-level equivalents (9 for ninth grade, 10 for tenth grade, etc.) on the basis of national norms, and the scores were used to assign students to remedial classes. The median scores for these applicants, about to enter thirteenth grade, were as follows: word meaning, 11.3; language usage, 10.4; spelling, 10.2; paragraph meaning, 10.1; arithmetic reasoning, 9.5; arithmetic computation, 8.4. The median scores for the transfer students alone did not vary greatly (plus or minus 0.4) from the figures above. Thus, on the basis of national norms, these scores indicate that the applicant clientele of the college had an achievement level equal to the first two years of high school. As a "cutting score for placement in remedial mathematics and English classes" [16] the college used the score of 9.4. On this basis, 20 to 30 per cent of the applicants fell in the remedial category on five of the six sections of the achievement test.[17] In sum, the college must base itself on a clientele low in scholastic achievement and college aptitude.

SOCIOECONOMIC BACKGROUND

This low-ability, transfer-oriented clientele can be more fully understood if a nonacademic element is considered. Differences among colleges in academic selectivity and cost of attending almost necessarily entail some social and economic differentiation of student bodies. A private university can be expected to have a social base different from that of a state university, which in turn is likely to have a student base somewhat different from that of a state college. A public junior college will almost surely

[16] *Ibid.*

[17] *Ibid.*

be different from a private university, but its difference from the state university and the state college is more problematic. Much depends on the geographic location of the junior college and the higher-education complex of which it is a part.

For the San Jose–San Francisco Bay area, a wide range of socioeconomic differences among college student bodies could be expected. The leading private university in this region is Stanford University, a high-cost school with high admission standards. It is 15 miles from San Jose. The University of California at Berkeley, a branch of the state university approximately 50 miles from San Jose, has similar academic selectivity but lower student costs. Its tuition is nominal, but most of its students have the expense of living away from home. The admission standards of the state university are at a level where only about 11 per cent of the high school graduates of the state qualify.[18] Quite different from admission to either of these two universities, for San Jose high school graduates, would be admission to San Jose State College or entry into the junior college. Both are tuition-free and close to the students' homes; admission standards are modest in the state college[19] and nonexistent in the junior college.

It was hypothesized that these four colleges would range from high to low in socioeconomic status of students drawn from the city of San Jose, the sharpest break occurring between the state university and the state college—a difference occasioned by selectivity, cost, and distance. From the records of these four

[18] *A Study of the Need for Additional Centers of Public Higher Education in California,* California State Department of Education, Sacramento, 1957, pp. 126–128; hereinafter cited as *Study of Need.* For the June, 1955, graduates from public high schools, the figure for the state as a whole was 11.4; for the San Jose metropolitan area (Santa Clara County) it was 12.8.

[19] In 1955, approximately 44 per cent of the high school graduates of the state met state college entrance requirements. In the San Jose metropolitan area, about 47 per cent qualified. *Ibid.*

colleges, information was obtained on freshman entrants from the city of San Jose.[20] Two indicators of socioeconomic background were used: the occupation of the student's father, and the economic level of the section of the city in which the student's family resided. Fathers' occupations reported by the students were categorized as (1) upper white collar (professionals, managers, proprietors, and officials); (2) lower white collar (sales, clerical, and kindred workers); (3) upper blue collar (craftsmen, foremen, and operatives); and (4) lower blue collar (service workers and laborers). These categories were also applied to the total working population of San Jose, as reported in the 1950 census. Table 5 shows the occupational distributions of the four colleges (San Jose entrants alone) and the city as a whole. The expected socioeconomic gradations can readily be seen. For Stanford, nearly nine out of ten students from San Jose came from families of professional men, business owners, and business officials,[21] with about 13 per cent from lower-white-collar or blue-collar homes. The distribution for the state university shows a greater spread, approximately 31 per cent of the students from San Jose coming from lower-white-collar or blue-collar homes. The state college and junior college, in turn, had about 62 and 77 per cent, respectively, from other than professional or business background. The largest difference in the percentage of students from the top occupational category was between the state university and the state college (31 per cent),

[20] The collection and preliminary analysis of these data were done by David Nasatir, then a graduate student at Stanford University. For methodological details see Appendix 2.

[21] The findings of this study, while based on San Jose students alone, approximate those based on the Stanford student body as a whole. A study of Stanford male seniors made in 1956 showed that approximately 84 per cent were from upper-white-collar background. Approximately 8 per cent were "white-collar rank and file," and 8 per cent were from blue-collar families. Information supplied by Fred Chino from an unpublished manuscript.

Table 5

Comparison of Four Colleges* by Occupation of Student's Father

(In per cent)

College	Upper-white-collar	Lower-white-collar	Upper-blue-collar	Lower-blue-collar	Total
Stanford University	87	7	6	0	100 (*N* = 55)†
University of California	69	14	11	6	100 (*N* = 52)
San Jose State College	38	17	29	16	100 (*N* = 147)
San Jose Junior College	23	15	45	17	100 (*N* = 95)
City of San Jose‡	26	17	38	19	100 (*N* = 23,699)

* Based on freshmen students from city of San Jose; see Appendix 2.

† *N* means number of cases.

‡ Employed males, fourteen years and over (occupation reported), San Jose as "urban place," 1950 census.

SOURCES: College records and U.S. Bureau of the Census, *Census of Population: 1950*, vol. II, *Characteristics of the Population*, California, 1952, part 5, p. 122.

the second largest difference was between the state university and Stanford (18 per cent), and the smallest difference was between the state college and the junior college (15 per cent).

For convenience in comparing the occupational distributions of the several colleges with the occupational composition of the city as a whole, the information in Table 5 is represented in ratio form in Table 6. Percentages are compared, with a ratio of 1

Table 6
Ratio of Occupational Composition*
of College Student Body†
and City of San Jose

College	Occupation of father			
	Upper-white-collar	Lower-white-collar	Upper-blue-collar	Lower-blue-collar
Stanford University	3.3	0.4	0.1	0.0
University of California	2.6	0.8	0.3	0.3
San Jose State College	1.4	1.0	0.8	0.9
San Jose Junior College	0.9	0.9	1.2	0.9

* College percentage compared to percentage of same occupational category in the city of San Jose (see Table 5). Ratio of 1 means same percentage in college as in city; greater than 1, a larger college percentage; less than 1, a smaller percentage in the college distribution than in the city.

† Based on freshmen students from city of San Jose; see Appendix 2.

SOURCES: College records and U.S. Bureau of the Census, *Census of Population: 1950*, vol. II, *Characteristics of the Population*, California, 1952, part 5, p. 122.

meaning an identical distribution for the college and the city.[22] Scores of over 1 indicate an overrepresentation in the college and ratios of less than 1, an underrepresentation. As can be seen, the state college is not too dissimilar to the city at large, and the junior college has a clientele base virtually identical with the city-wide occupational structure. The junior college exceeds the city distribution only in the category of skilled and semiskilled workmen, which accounted for 45 per cent of its student body.

[22] For a similar index of socioeconomic representation, see Raymond A. Mulligan, "Socio-economic Background and College Enrollment," *American Sociological Review*, vol. 16, no. 2, pp. 188–196, April, 1951.

Thus, indexed by father's occupation, the junior college is relatively a "working-class" college. Less than a fourth of its students from the city of San Jose come from business and professional families, while two out of three had a blue-collar background. This characterization is strengthened when it is considered that more upper-class and upper-middle-class youths go to college than those from the lower-class levels. If the college-going population were spread evenly, each college should be expected to have a heavy representation from the upper-income groups. Thus, a distribution of students that follows the class distribution in the city is a disproportionate representation from the lower-income groups, in terms of the college-going population. Clearly an extensive democratization of higher education is involved, with access to some form of higher education relatively unhindered by income level.

The predominantly blue-collar selection that the college obtains from the college entrants of the city is not produced by its terminal programs, although the effect of the vocational curricula is in that direction. As Table 7 shows, 60 per cent of the students with transfer intention came from blue-collar families, compared to 68 per cent among the terminal students. The want-to-go-to-college attitude is operative across socioeconomic levels in the junior college, and economic background does not impel students into "heads" and "hands" majors in the college.

The second indicator of socioeconomic background provides a similar picture. From street addresses, students were located as to the geographic area of the city within which their families resided. The general economic status of these city areas was determined by means of an urban typology that had previously been applied to San Jose (see Appendix 2), and the areas were grouped into four categories of high to low status. Table 8 shows the way in which the four colleges and the city as a whole were distributed in these status-of-area categories. It can be seen that

Table 7
Comparison of Transfer and Terminal Students
of San Jose Junior College
by Occupation of Father
(In per cent)

Curriculum	Occupation of father: Upper-white-collar	Lower-white-collar	Upper-blue-collar	Lower-blue-collar	Total
Transfer	26	14	44	16	100 (N = 70)
Terminal	16	16	48	20	100 (*N* = 25)
Entire college	23	15	45	17	100 (*N* = 95)
Difference between transfer and terminal	10	2	4	4	

SOURCE: San Jose Junior College records.

the first three colleges drew heavily from high-status neighborhoods, while the student constituency of the junior college was spread representatively across the social areas of the city.

Thus it may be seen that the clientele of the junior college drawn from its own city was markedly different from that drawn by a private university and a state university, both located nearby, and to a lesser extent was different from a closely located state college. The junior college approached the representative distribution of students one would expect to find in a com-

Table 8

Comparison of Four Colleges* by Economic Status of Student's Home Neighborhood

(In per cent)

College	Neighborhood status				Total
	High	Medium-high	Medium-low	Low	
Stanford University	71	16	4	9	100 (*N* = 55)
University of California	75	21	4	0	100 (*N* = 52)
San Jose State College	51	24	16	9	100 (*N* = 147)
San Jose Junior College	30	25	27	18	100 (*N* = 95)
City of San Jose	29	26	27	18	100 (*N* = 95,280)

* Based on freshmen students from city of San Jose; see Appendix 2.

SOURCES: College records and Stephen T. Boggs, "Social Areas of San Jose," unpublished manuscript.

prehensive high school. How did this come about? It is known that the entire output of nearby high schools does not appear at the junior college. Of the June, 1955, high school graduates in the San Jose metropolitan area, less than one-fifth continued their education in a junior college.[23] The spread of the junior college distribution results from several selective factors that largely balance one another. Low-income students undoubtedly do not proceed past high school in proportion to their numbers, even with tuition-free colleges on the scene. Personal economic

[23] See Table 9 below.

barriers exist for many of them, because going to a school represents a potential loss to family income and motivation to go to college will be in many cases less strongly developed than in their high-income counterparts. Therefore, even a public junior college should generally be somewhat more top-heavy in socioeconomic distribution than the San Jose Junior College. At the same time, however, students of high socioeconomic status are more likely to proceed to private colleges and the state university, reducing the potential junior college enrollment from the higher-income groups. In this way some underattraction at the lower end of the socioeconomic ladder may be roughly offset by low attraction of those at the upper end, producing for the college a social base that is closely representative of the economic composition of the city.

Other public junior colleges do not necessarily have clienteles similar in socioeconomic characteristics to that of San Jose Junior College. Suburban and metropolitan junior colleges may vary considerably in the socioeconomic composition of their student bodies. Probably, however, public junior colleges typically come closer to approximating the socioeconomic distributions of nearby populations than do other forms of college organization. Relatively few barriers—social, economic, or academic—intervene between the prospective student and the junior college. In the nonselective college there is relatively little to prevent an across-the-board "draw" from the local population.

This comparative picture suggests that in states with complex systems of higher education the question, Who goes to college? needs to be supplemented by the question, To which of the major types of colleges? With unlimited access to the junior college and only modestly limited access to the state college, the most important socioeconomic distinctions may well be found increasingly within higher education rather than between college and noncollege. As educational opportunity becomes available close at home for more students, the crucial difference may be be-

Table 9
Public High School Graduates, June, 1955,
Continuing Their Education in California
(By type of college)

Type of college	High school graduates		
	San Jose*		California†
	Number	Per cent	Per cent
State college	563	22.6	9.4
Junior college	460	18.5	24.6
State university	62	2.5	4.4
Private college	104	4.2	4.7
All colleges	1,189	47.8	43.0

* San Jose Metropolitan Area, or Santa Clara County.

† Based on data from forty-one selected California counties; included were 41,423 high school graduates, more than half of the total number in the state.

SOURCE: *A Study of the Need for Additional Centers of Public Higher Education in California,* California State Department of Education, Sacramento, 1957, pp. 130–131.

tween the relatively small group of students who go away from home for a college education and the larger commuting group. In this regard, an unanticipated problem in gathering data was that only a few students from the graduating classes of the San Jose high schools proceed directly to Stanford University or the University of California at Berkeley.[24] Table 9 shows that for the entire San Jose metropolitan area (Santa Clara County), only 2.5 per cent of high school graduates in June, 1955, proceeded to the state university and only 4.2 per cent to all private

[24] See Appendix 2.

colleges, a total of less than 7 per cent. The corresponding figures for the state as a whole were 4.4 per cent and 4.7 per cent, or together only slightly more than 9 per cent. At the same time, more than 40 per cent of the high school graduates from the San Jose metropolitan area were at a state college or a junior college, nearly all, undoubtedly, being at San Jose State College or San Jose Junior College. The state college percentage for the San Jose metropolitan area greatly exceeds that for the state as a whole, 22.6 per cent compared to 9.4 per cent, indicating that San Jose State pulled students from all other categories. San Jose high school graduates continue their education in the local area.

The establishment of conveniently placed colleges means that most college students will remain at home, and socioeconomic differentiation then arises between the colleges of local draw and the colleges with state and national recruitment. The intervening opportunities presented by the nearby colleges apparently keep most students from going far afield in search of a college education, especially for the first two years of college. The hypothesis is offered that a growing system of locally and regionally oriented colleges will result in maintaining and probably increasing the socioeconomic differentiation of clienteles among colleges. In the process of increasing educational opportunity, these local colleges transform the differential between those who go to college and those who do not into a differential between those who go away from home to the more expensive and generally more selective colleges and those who attend schools at home which are less expensive and usually less selective. Since all major urban areas of California have one or more state colleges and one or more junior colleges, this is probably a common differential in the state. It is also probable in those parts of the country which have a similar higher-education pattern, namely, locally oriented as well as state and nationally oriented units.

THE STUDENT TRAFFIC

After this review of the students' background, a discussion of their passage through the college suggests itself. How long do students stay, how many graduate, and how many transfer to other colleges? In answering such questions, the primary interest will not be in the impact of a junior college on its students but in the impact of the students on the college. It has already been pointed out that the college has an unselected student body relatively low in academic ability. These features, one expects, will shape the character of a college. But in what direction and by what specific means?

Characteristic of the college's student body is heavy turnover in membership. This shows, first, in the rate of leaving. The total loss of students during any period of time from a junior college includes graduates, transfers, and dropouts. Table 10 shows student losses by semester, the loss figures representing the difference between the total enrollment of one semester and the returning enrollment of the following term. The loss figures include midsemester as well as between-semester losses; the figures also show what happened during the middle of the academic year as well as between one year and the next. As can be seen, the number of students leaving the college during the first half of the academic year, sometime during the fall semester or before the spring semester is fully under way, approximated 30 per cent: 34 per cent the first year, followed by 28 per cent, 30 per cent, and 31 per cent in the next three years. This means that nearly one out of every three students enrolled in the fall semester of an academic year had left in the second semester. This September-to-February loss exceeded five hundred students a year in the third and fourth years. Then, the number of students leaving the college for any reason during the spring semester or between the spring term and the following fall was

Table 10

Student Losses, San Jose Junior College, 1953–1954 to 1956–1957

Semester interval	Enrollment		Student loss	
	Beginning*	Returning†	Number	Per cent
Fall, 1953–spring, 1954	580	383	197	34
Spring, 1954–fall, 1954	653	305	348	53
Fall, 1954–spring, 1955	1,415	1,025	390	28
Spring, 1955–fall, 1955	1,571	674	897	57
Fall, 1955–spring, 1956	1,855	1,306	549	30
Spring, 1956–fall, 1956	1,838	823	1,015	55
Fall, 1956–spring, 1957	2,133	1,463	670	31

* Total enrollment of the first of the two semesters.

† Number of students of the first semester that returned the succeeding semester.

SOURCE: San Jose Junior College, Division of Student Services files, San Jose Unified School District.

more than 50 per cent of the spring enrollment: 53 per cent between the first and second years, 57 per cent between the second and third, and 55 per cent between the third and fourth. Of the students on the campus at midyear, about one out of two have thus disappeared the following fall. The number of students in this February-to-September loss exceeded one thousand between the third and fourth years. A large number of students, then, stay at the college for a short time only, and the turnover is rapid.

The inflow of students was increased because the college received a large number of new students at the academic midyear as well as at the beginning of each academic year. As Table 4 shows, spring enrollment of the college exceeded fall enrollment in each of the first three years, despite the considerable midyear losses mentioned above. The students that left were replaced by roughly 250 new ones in the middle of the first year, 500 in each of the second and third years, and 400 in the middle of the fourth year. Thus, the midyear additions were of the magnitude of the midyear losses. With the growth of the college between academic years, it is also clear that the new students at the beginning of each year have numbered more than the between-year losses. The new untutored students in the fall numbered a half to two-thirds of the total student body each year. The magnitude of these additions, when considered together with the extensive losses, makes it clear that student membership shifted rapidly. The turnover exceeded anything commonly found in the high school or in the traditional forms of college organization.

A larger change-over of students than in four-year schools and colleges could be expected because of the short two-year span of the junior college. But the rapid flow noted above was occasioned only in part by the two-year span; most students did not complete two years of work. The loss figures in Table 10 suggest much early leaving. Incompletion is more directly indicated by figures showing how many students completed two years. Nearly 3,700 students entered the college for full-time study by the beginning of its third year; with normal progress, these students could have graduated by the end of the fourth year. The number who graduated with an associate in arts degree was 26 at the end of the first year (students who had entered with advanced standing), 144 the second year, 230 the third, and 204 the fourth, or a total of 604 students, which is fewer than one-sixth of the number of entering students.[25]

[25] This is not unique, because junior college students generally do not graduate. One state report for 1952 showed a 66 per cent loss between the first and second year in California junior colleges; this suggests that the loss by the end of the second year would be in the 75-to-85 per cent range. *Restudy*, p. 115. Nationally, about one-third of the number of entering junior college students graduate. See Medsker, *op. cit.*, chap. 4.

As for those who proceeded to other colleges, before or after receiving the associate in arts degree, an analysis of the students who entered the college at the beginning of the third year (1955–1956) showed that 285 out of 1,181, or 24.1 per cent, later transferred.[26] The transferring students constituted one-third of the students who had entered into transfer programs. At first glance these proportions seem unduly low. They reflect a general phenomenon of the California junior college, however, as may be seen in comparative figures for the state as a whole. A 1955 state study[27] indicated that:

> The number of junior college students who will actually transfer to four-year institutions constitutes a relatively small proportion of the total number enrolled in the junior colleges. The Office of Relations with Schools of the University of California has reported that "a 50 per cent sample of California public junior colleges indicates that while 66 per cent of their entrants state that they expect to transfer later to four-year colleges, only about a third of these actually do transfer."

A third who actually transfer, of the 66 per cent who are transfer majors, totals about 22 per cent of all entering students. This parallels the San Jose figure, for there, too, about one-third of transfer-intentioned students actually transfer; this is about 25 per cent of all entering students.

Transferring students commonly move out of the college after a relatively short stay. This is shown in several ways. An analysis of transcripts of student records sent to other colleges at the request of students in the college showed that 23 per cent were for students with the associate in arts degree. The remaining 77 per cent did not have the degree, and 52 per cent of all requests for transcripts were for students who had completed one year

[26] San Jose Junior College, Division of Student Services, report dated Dec. 3, 1957.

[27] *Restudy*, p. 116.

of work or less.[28] Of the 749 students who actually transferred to the nearby San Jose State College during the junior college's first 3½ years, 211, or 28 per cent, were graduates of the junior college and 538, or 72 per cent, were not.[29] These 749 students spent, on the average, 2.3 semesters in the junior college before transferring. The typical stay in the college of the student with a transfer destiny, then, was between a year and a year and a half.

That the transfer students went primarily to the nearby state college is indicated by the fact that two out of three requested transcripts were for this one college, ten times as many as were for the University of California at Berkeley which was the next most popular destination.[30] The state college's share of the admitted, rather than the applying, students would be even greater, because its proximity would be facilitating, its admission policy is well known to the local students and hence acceptance could be better predicted, and its requirements are not so high as those of the more selective colleges. In its transfer output, San Jose Junior College is primarily a feeder station for this one college.

How well do the transferring students do at the state college? The grade-point differential for the 749 transferring students was as follows, a 2 being equal to a C average: last semester at

[28] San Jose Junior College, Division of Student Services, Transcripts Sent during Summer, 1956, August, 1956.

[29] San Jose Junior College, Division of Student Services, Summary of Records Made after Transfer to San Jose State College by Students of San Jose Junior College, Dec. 23, 1957.

[30] San Jose Junior College, Division of Student Services, Transcripts Sent during Summer, 1956, August, 1956. Of the 456 transcripts sent, 305 went to San Jose State College and 29 to the University of California. The total number of students that actually transferred from San Jose Junior College to other colleges is not known, because acceptance by the senior college or university is not always acknowledged and the college's records were incomplete.

San Jose Junior College, 2.3 average grade-point average; first semester at San Jose State College, 1.8; third semester, 2.1.[31] The transferring students therefore averaged about C+ at the junior college; their grades slipped one-half a grade point (−0.5) the first semester after transferring and then rose in the third semester to 0.2 lower than junior college grades. The transfer students were, on the average, failing in their first semester at the state college (below a C average) but by the third semester, were performing at a passing level. These students enrolled predominantly in three majors: business (201, or 26.8 per cent of all transferring students); teaching (198, or 26.4 per cent); and engineering and mathematics (96, or 12.8 per cent).[32]

The picture of the junior college as closely related to the nearby state college in its academic output can be further elaborated. Students also transfer in the opposite direction; some students that fail at the state college later appear at the junior college. This occurred each semester of the academic year but particularly after the fall term when some state college entrants failed. So many reverse-flow students were received at the beginning of each spring semester that the junior college predicted its enrollment for the last half of the academic year on the basis of "first our own current enrollment and second, whatever information we may obtain from San Jose State with reference to potential eliminations at the close of the fall quarter."[33] With this two-way traffic between the two colleges, San Jose Junior College was clearly taking care of marginal state college students. In this pattern, many of the failing students want to return to San Jose State College, if and when they can requalify. Of the

[31] San Jose Junior College, Division of Student Services, Summary of Records Made after Transfer to San Jose State College by Students of San Jose Junior College, Dec. 23, 1957.

[32] *Ibid.*

[33] San Jose Junior College, Outline of Procedure for Schedule Construction undated memorandum.

749 students referred to previously as having transferred from the junior college to the state college, 214, or 28.6 per cent, had been at San Jose State College before enrolling at the junior college.[34] For these students, as well as for those sent "down" who never return to the state college, the junior college plays a role similar to that of the pre–1953 unit under state college administration. It operates essentially as an extension division, a detour from which failing state college students hope to return to the main road after a semester or two of work. In a sense, this segment of the junior college's transfer output consists of students that are not its own.

With the college's transfer output amounting to about one-fourth of its students, what happens to the rest of the student body? As seen in Table 4, another fourth of the students were enrolled in terminal programs.[35] The remaining one-half is important, posing for the college special problems of student participation and destiny.

THE LATENT TERMINAL STUDENT

It has been indicated that, as a new junior college, the San Jose institution was committed to the admission of all applicants and to an unrestricted choice of curriculum by the entering student. The question may now be raised as to what these commitments entail for college management. As previously seen, the entering students were oriented toward transfer; at the same time they proved to have low academic aptitude and many had poor

[34] San Jose Junior College, Division of Student Services, Summary of Records Made after Transfer to San Jose State College by Students of San Jose Junior College, Dec. 23, 1957.

[35] For the state as a whole, the terminal enrollment is about one-third and the two categories mentioned above total about 55 per cent of junior college students. *Restudy*, p. 116.

achievement records in high school. The resulting disparity between the desire and the capability of many students meant that the college was faced with the alternative of either allowing students of low promise to complete junior college work and transfer elsewhere or denying them the opportunity to transfer. The first alternative is easier to accept in day-to-day operation because it smoothes relationships with students, but it is not promising for the academic reputation of the institution. If a junior college allows students of low academic promise to slip through, then the frequency of failure by transfer students at senior colleges will increase. The reputation and self-respect of the staff members are also affected. A teacher of the college said, in interview, "I do not want my transfer students making B with me, then D at State or Cal." The performance of transfer students has personal as well as organizational interest. The college has a stake in seeing that many prospective transfer students of little promise are retained in the college's own jurisdiction. The student who cannot or will not perform at the "college level," *as this is defined by other colleges,* needs to be convinced that he is not capable of undertaking a more extended college education.

Caught between its own open door and the standards of other colleges, therefore, an unselective two-year college needs to "administer" the student who is, in fact, destined to be a terminal student but who does not know it or refuses to recognize this likelihood at the time of entry. The person who earmarks himself as a terminal student is no special problem, nor is the candidate for transfer who comes with high scholastic promise. For the pure terminal and the pure transfer students, destiny is in line with intention. The procedure-shaping type of student is the latent terminal, the "overintender" whose transfer status as student belies his terminal future.

Before the junior college opened its doors, administrators of the San Jose district were aware of this type of student. A planning committee in 1952 said:[36]

> Special consideration should be given those students with fewer than five recommending units from high school and who indicate a desire to follow a transfer program. Experience in other institutions indicates that most of these students will not be successful in a transfer program, and should, if possible, be counseled into a terminal offering. Still, it would seem that many will want a try at a transfer program and should be given that chance.

A student with fewer than five recommending units from high school would not be eligible for any college that has some degree of selectivity, including the nearby state college. When such students transfer from junior colleges, they are often categorized by senior colleges and universities as "ineligibles," referring to the fact that they were not eligible for direct admission at the time of their high school graduation. The University of California makes a distinction between eligible and ineligible transfer students, both in considering applications of transfer students and in studying their later academic performance. Having learned that the ineligibles do less well, on the average, at the university, the university exacts a higher admission requirement at the time of transfer. The ineligibles are not a promising group of college students, and the senior colleges are aware of this. Although some ineligibles are able to transfer later, doing better in the junior college than in the high school or at least pulling a C average, most will not be successful in what they are trying to do, as pointed out by the district study committee. Still, they are not prevented from attempting a transfer program; despite poor

[36] *Report of the Junior College Sub-committee on General Education,* San Jose Unified School District, Nov. 12, 1952. A recommending unit is a grade of A or B in a subject taken for one year in grades 10, 11, or 12.

high school performance, the student who wants to try transfer work is given that chance. This policy is in line with a permissive orientation in the public schools and with the belief that there are students with ability who may do poorly in high school and yet be salvaged by the junior college.

The district committee did not specify how these students should be treated, other than suggesting that they "should, if possible, be counseled into a terminal program." In the operation of the college, several successive devices are used. While the early steps in this sequence apply to all students and only later ones to transfer students in academic trouble, all steps become most meaningful when interpreted as devices for managing the latent terminal. How can a student who is going to fail the transfer work be made to realize this? An early step is the preentrance testing reported earlier in this chapter. Low scores on achievement tests lead to remedial classes; for example, "Transfer students who fall below 9.0 grade placement in the English test in any area are required to enroll in Sub-Freshman English." [37] Assignment to remedial work casts doubt on the promise of some latent terminals and slows their movement toward the bona fide courses. In addition, an objective record begins to accumulate, as all test scores are made part of a counseling folder. A second step is an interview with a counselor, before the beginning of each semester, for purposes of class scheduling. "At this interview the counselor assists the student to choose the proper courses in light of his objectives, his test scores, the high school record and test records from his previous schools."[38] The assistance is initially gentle. A common case is the student who wants to be an engineer but whose test scores and school grades indicate that he is a nearly hopeless candidate. Said one counselor, "I never

[37] *San Jose Junior College Handbook for Counselors, 1957–1958,* San Jose Unified School District, San Jose, p. 2.

[38] *Ibid.*

openly countermand his choice, but edge him toward a terminal program by gradually laying out the facts of life." Counselors can become more severe later in the sequence when they have grades as a talking point and the student is in trouble. In initial counseling, student choice still has great weight.

The college works somewhat more actively, although indirectly, against the latent terminal in a specially devised course entitled "Psychology 5, Orientation to College." This one-unit mandatory course may be seen as a third step in the sequence of devices for reorienting the student who is in over his head. All sections of the course are taught by the counseling staff—teachers who have a part-time counseling assignment. A major purpose of the course is "to assist students in evaluating their own abilities, interests, and aptitudes; in assaying their vocational choices in light of this evaluation; and in making educational plans to implement their choices." [39] The course is divided into four sections: first, "orientation to the college," with three class hours suggested for coverage; second, "how to study," four hours being recommended. A third section is "vocational opportunities and choices," with five class hours suggested. Here occupational opportunities are discussed and more testing is accomplished. Among the tests are the "Lee Thorpe Interest Inventory given to all students for motivating a self-appraisal of vocational choice" and the "Strong Interest Inventory for all who are undecided about choice or who show disparity between accomplishment and vocational choice." [40] Mechanical and clerical aptitude tests are also taken by all. Then an "occupational paper [is] required of all students for [their] chosen occupation." [41] Here the student learns the duties and responsibilities of the kind of job he desires, the training and education required, and makes

[39] *Ibid.*, p. 3.

[40] *Ibid.*, pp. 5–6.

[41] *Ibid.*, p. 6.

a "self-appraisal of fitness for job in the light of test scores, grades, employment experience, health, finances, age, and drive." [42]

These tests and papers are then used in class discussion and individual interviews. In this class, the counselees themselves arrange and work with a Counselor's Folder and a Student Test Profile. By their handling of their own records, they are more closely confronted with test data and the recommendations of teachers and counselors. This procedure is intended to heighten the student's awareness of his own capacity in relation to educational and occupational choices and particularly to strike at the latent terminal student. Repeatedly the teacher-counselors are advised by the college to "be alert to the problem of unrealistic vocational goals," and with this, to "help students to accept their limitations and strive for success in other worthwhile objectives that are within their grasp." [43] Counselors reported in interview that it was particularly in this course that they were able to talk freely to the students about the disparity between personal objective and capacity. The orientation class was considered a good place "to talk tough," and to explain in an impersonal way the facts of life for the "hopeless" transfer student.

Following this vocational counseling, "Psychology 5" concludes with a fourth section of approximately four class hours on "building an educational program." Here students plan their program for later semesters, study the lower-division requirements of the college to which they hope to transfer, and consider such additional hurdles as the college entrance examinations required by other colleges.

If he wishes, the latent terminal student can ignore the advice he receives up to this point. While he is in the counseling course, during his first semester, he is also engaged in other course work.

[42] *Ibid.*, p. 6.

[43] *Ibid.*, p. 10.

He may wait to see what happens to him. Probably counseling alone will not shut off his hope of going as far as possible. Realistic deterrence actually begins in the regular classes. Here the student is divested of any expectations that may linger from high school that he will be automatically passed and transferred. Then, if he receives low grades, he is thrown back into the counseling orbit by referral from the classroom to the counseling office. In a fourth step of the reorientation process, the evidence of actual accomplishment begins to go against him and an adverse record accumulates:[44]

> *Need for Improvement Notices* are issued by instructors to students who are doing unsatisfactory work. The carbon copy of the notice is given to the counselor who will be available for conference with the student. The responsibility lies with the student to see his counselor. However, experience shows that some counselees are unable to be sufficiently self-directive to seek aid. The counselor should, in such cases, send for the student using the Request for Conference blank. If the student fails to respond to the Request for Conference slip, this may become a disciplinary matter and should be referred to the deans.
>
> After a conference has been held, the Need for Improvement notices are filed in the student's folder. *This may be important* in case of a complaint concerning the fairness of a final grade.

Again the procedure leads the student to self-assessment and the carbon-copy routine insures that if he does not seek advice, the advice will seek him. All the paper work has a good reason. As put in an unpublished report of the college, the problems of the latent terminal student require "skillful and delicate handling. An accumulation of pertinent factual information may serve to fortify the objectivity of the student-counselor relationship."

[44] *Ibid.*, p. 20. Italics in the original.

A fifth step for many in the process of discouragement is the placing of a student on probation:[45]

> Students [whose] grade point averages fall below 2.0 in any semester will, upon recommendation by the Scholarship Committee, be placed on probationary standing. Students whose grade point averages fall below 2.0 for the second semester are placed on second probation. Students who fail to make a 2.0 grade point average the ensuing semester may be advised to withdraw from the college.

Clearly the college is reluctant to do anything so drastic with the probationary student as to drop him entirely, for as can be seen above, he can continue in this status for three consecutive semesters before he may be advised to withdraw. Some teachers complain that "anyone can enter, fail, and continue to do so indefinitely."[46] The purpose of probation in this context, however, is not to provide a status halfway out of the college but, as stated in the unpublished report, to "assist the student to seek an objective (major field) at a level on which he can succeed." The real meaning of probation lies in its killing off the hope of some of the latent terminal students. A "transfer student must have a C (2.0) grade point average to be eligible for the A.A. degree,"[47] whereas no minimum average is set for terminal students. More important, other colleges require a C average or better for the transfer student; he must also remain in the junior college for a specified number of units if he has had a poor high school record. For San Jose State: "A student must have a grade point average of 2.0 (C) in order to be eligible to transfer and must have completed 24 units of junior

[45] *Ibid.*

[46] A response to a questionnaire item on what teachers like least about working in a junior college. Junior college questionnaire will be later discussed.

[47] *San Jose Junior College Handbook for Counselors, 1957–58, op. cit.*, p. 23.

college work if they were ineligible to attend San Jose State at the time of high school graduation." [48] And for the University of California: "Students who were ineligible to attend the University on the basis of high school grades must complete 30 units in junior college with a grade point average of . . . 2.8 on the C = 2 grade point basis." [49] Numerically, probation was no light matter in the college. Thirty per cent of all students enrolled at the end of the spring semester, 1955–1956, and returning in the fall of 1956–1957, were on probation. Seventy-seven per cent of these probationary students were in a transfer program.[50]

This sequence applies strictly only to the failing student. For him, the open door of the college leads into a funnel. Similarly, but to a lesser degree, students who are barely passing find themselves squeezed toward a redefinition of their occupational and academic future. Along the way, teacher-counselors urge the latent terminal student to give up his transfer intention, and they stand ready to console him in accepting a terminal curriculum. The effect of the drawn out counseling procedure when it operates effectively is never to say a final "no," but to move the student into a position where it finally seems best to him to declare himself out of the transfer competition.

Whether or not this sequence operates effectively in managing latent terminal students depends on various factors, such as severity in grading. But the series of counseling devices is only one of a number of adaptations that the junior college makes in facing the existence of large numbers of latent terminal students. In itself it reflects the heightened importance of counseling and guidance. The task of reorienting students is of such magnitude that it cannot be handled by a counseling staff ap-

[48] *Ibid.*, p. 27.

[49] *Ibid.*, p. 29.

[50] San Jose Junior College, Digest of Analysis of the Records of 468 Students Placed on Probation for the Fall Semester, 1956, Sept. 3, 1956.

pended to instructional personnel and operating only in a separate counseling office. Counseling is brought into the classroom, particularly in order to shadow the student who has assigned himself to failure.

The importance of counseling in the minds of the college's teachers and administrators was reflected in the results of a questionnaire circulated among the staff.[51] To the question "In your judgment, what *should be* the importance of junior college educational and vocational counseling (not merely scheduling) in comparison with instruction?" 10 per cent of the staff answered that it was more important than instruction, 70 per cent that it was equally as important, and 20 per cent that it was less important. Thus, 80 per cent saw it as of equal or greater importance than instruction—a response not likely to be duplicated in four-year colleges and universities. Then, too, only 11 per cent of the staff agreed with the statement, proposed in another question, that "students are frequently 'over-counseled' in a junior college." Apparently the staff members regard the extensive counseling effort as appropriate.

The difficulty of getting students to accept a terminal designation and graduating after two years in a terminal program is suggested by the number of terminal students receiving an associate in arts degree. In the college's fourth year (1956–1957), 204 students received an A.A. degree; 133, or 65 per cent, were tagged as transfer students; and 71, or 35 per cent, were called terminal. This terminal two-year output of 71 was from a student body numbering nearly 2,000, of which more than a third (between 700 and 800) had second-year standing. Of the 71 students, 20 had an electronics major, 22 were in "other shops," 23 in some business field, and 6 had a general education major.[52]

[51] See Appendix 1.

[52] San Jose Junior College, Division and Major of All Graduates, June 17, 1957.

Table 11

Job Placement of Students of San Jose Junior College, 1953–1954 to 1955–1956

Type of work	Students placed	
	Number*	Per cent
Technical:		
Television repairman	51	36
Electronic technician	26	19
Other technical	17	12
White-collar:		
Office worker	21	15
Salesman	10	7
Other white-collar	9	7
Other	6	4
Total	140	100

* Does not include all students who found work after junior college training. Records on students placed by the college were incomplete and students also place themselves after graduating or dropping out.

SOURCE: San Jose Junior College, Division of Student Services.

The college prepares students directly for the fields suggested by the majors above. The college's job-placement records for its first three years (Table 11) showed that about two out of three placements were technicians; more than a half of the placements were for television repairmen and other electronics technicians. Outside of technical fields, students were placed primarily in office work and in selling. Although the numbers reported in Table 11 are incomplete, they are sufficient to indicate the relationship of the college to the occupational structure of its area.

The terminal graduate goes into employment as a technician or office worker.

In addition to extensive effort in counseling, the administering of the latent terminal student also calls for an appropriate curriculum structure. The change from transfer to terminal status can be expedited if the student moves toward the completion of a terminal major while attempting transfer work. Toward this end, he can be requested to take terminal courses as electives. The college also constructed dual-purpose curricula, with courses that satisfy both transfer and terminal requirements and that cater to both kinds of students. Typifying the tendency to fuse curricula is the following statement of requirements for general majors:[53]

> The requirements of the General Major—A.A. only—are similar to those of the General Major—A.A. with A.B. or B.S. transfer, although they are not identical. They are similar enough, however, so that the student who may decide to alter his transfer objective can—with minor modifications of his original educational plan—readily complete the requirements for the A.A. degree.

The transfer general major is popular with the student body, because it is recommended by the college to students wishing to enter teaching, social science, journalism, law, and numerous other fields. In 1956, 26 per cent of the college's enrollment appeared in this major; at the same time the terminal general major was chosen by less than 4 per cent of the students. A student may formally remain a transfer student, while proceeding in fact toward a terminal goal. This means that the latent terminal student, during most of his time in college, never need appear as a true terminal. Unless his grades are unduly low, he may com-

[53] *San Jose Junior College Bulletin, 1956–57,* San Jose Unified School District, San Jose, Calif., 1956, p. 46.

plete the A.A. degree, graduate from the college still designated as a transfer student, and then simply not enter another college. If his performance becomes highly unsatisfactory, he can be redesignated as a terminal major "with minor modifications" late in his stay at the college. In either case, the integrated curriculum has the latent function of providing face saving and status for the student during the time spent in the college.

The tendency to fuse is obviously directly opposite to the making of sharp distinctions between types of curricula and types of students. Clear distinctions complicate the movement of students within the organization, especially where most changes run counter to the original desires of students and move students from curricula of higher to those of lower standing. Their path is smoothed if the transfer and terminal "tracks" are not kept entirely separate. In one case in California, the public junior college has done away with the transfer and terminal distinction entirely, attempting to place all students on "one track."

Teachers and administrators alike stressed in interviews that many students try to avoid the terminal label even when they are aware that they are not likely to go on beyond the junior college. The college tends to keep the latent terminal students in the same classrooms as the pure transfers. The participation of the bona fide transfer student extensively overlaps that of the student who will not proceed past the college. The pure terminal students are also mixed in classes with the students designated as transfer. The vocational students have some shop classes that are for them alone, but in such courses as English, history, political science, and economics, they are together with transfer students. Unless mixed in this way, the terminal students become expensive through duplication of courses. But their entry into a common classroom adds to the diversity of ability and outlook faced by instructors, and over-all class ability is lowered. As mentioned earlier, the terminal students are markedly lower in academic ability, having, for example, at one time a median aptitude score of 12 compared to 36 for the transfer students. With the "shop" students of the college generally poorly equipped for the life of study, their addition to the common classroom increases the pressure on college level standards that is, in the first instance, occasioned by the latent terminal student. The triple-function classroom—for pure terminal, the latent terminal, and the true transfer student—confronts the teacher with a choice of either holding the work to a content and level desired by other colleges or changing it to take into account the terminal fate of the majority of the students. When educational standards are discussed in the college, this situation is generally the background. The only discussion of educational standards in the college's *Faculty Handbook*[54] is limited to this situation:

> In each course a reasonable standard of college-level performance is required. Through effective counseling, every attempt will be made to place students in the proper courses. However, students in programs leading only to the Associate in Arts degree will often be found in programs leading to transfer to a baccalaureate institution. In these cases, it is important to hold to a standard of performance which is governed by the course rather than by the student enrollment. There is no separate grading policy for Transfer and A.A. students.

The advice given the faculty here is to hold to the standards of transfer courses as if they were for pure transfer students only. All students are to be graded on a single scale. Logically, this would appear to make it very difficult for lower-ability students and would produce a large number of D's and F's in classes. However, the grade distributions for the college as a whole and most of its departments are on the high side of a nor-

[54] *San Jose Junior College Faculty Handbook, September, 1957,* San Jose Unified School District, San Jose, Calif., pp. 17–18.

mal distribution, that is, there are more A's and B's than D's and F's. The college does not grade with special severity. The dilemma is either to grade hard and fail large numbers in order to allow only those of ability to pass through the transfer courses, or to grade normal-to-easy, in which case lower-ability students may squeeze through. Wholesale failing results in fighting students and parents and is not an openly encouraged policy. It should be remembered, however, that 30 per cent of the students staying on for a sophomore year were on probation, that is, they had less than a C average. This indicates that grading was getting at large numbers of students. In some subjects, such as mathematics, physics, and biology, low grades were abundant.

The existence of the latent terminal student and the combining of transfer and terminal students in the comprehensive classroom means that the student who later goes on to other colleges takes his training alongside students of a lower ability than is found in selective colleges. One result from the questionnaire circulated among the college's staff is interesting in this regard. In response to a question asking whether they would prefer to have their own son attend a four-year college or a two-year college, 74 per cent of the staff preferred the senior college. The respondents were asked to explain why and in doing so they most frequently said that in the four-year college the caliber of the other students would be higher and the competition among students greater. Typical answers were: "he would be competing with a (scholastically) higher group"; "competition from a superior group"; "will compete with more brilliant students establishing higher standards"; "more competition with other competent students"; "the stimulation from students, faculty, and school atmosphere would be more outstanding. Facilities would be better and general academic stress would be greater"; "college and university classes can move faster in subject-matter areas."

The meaning of "college credit" is also changed in the handling of a junior college clientele. All course work of San Jose

Junior College, however terminal, is still considered work entitled to credit. As the school catalogue states: "All courses catalogued by San Jose Junior College are organized as junior college courses with appropriate standards of achievement and an accreditable assignment of credit-hour value. The satisfactory completion of any course will apply toward qualification for the Associate in Arts degree." [55] Thus, upon completion of a course, a student receives a form of credit. However, the credit received from certain terminal vocational courses is good only for the college's own associate in arts degree or for other junior colleges. It is not transferable to senior colleges, because they see "lower-division" credit in relation to four-year degrees. Therefore, the college has, in actuality, two forms of college credit: one that has general currency and one that is limited to junior colleges, which is, in practice, largely limited to the college itself. The latter is a new form of college credit that somewhat redefines the first two years of college. The courses that lead only to a terminal two-year degree are officially as much a part of college for the junior college as those that fit a four-year structure. The first two years of college credit, which in other kinds of colleges are understood as preparation for upper-division work, here become broadened in meaning to incorporate the terminal programs that are unique with the junior college.

The *needs* of the college to adapt to terminal students, latent and pure, who constitute an overwhelming majority of the student body, appear similar to those of most public high schools. The comprehensive secondary school is generally oriented to do something useful for students who do not proceed to college. The *response* of the college toward a fusion of students and programs, and away from sharp distinction and separation, also appears similar to the responses generally made to comprehensive high school student bodies. In contrast, a basic difference appears

[55] *San Jose Junior College Bulletin, 1956–57,* San Jose Unified School District, San Jose, Calif., 1956, p. 90.

when the situation of the junior college is compared with that of four-year colleges and universities. Most colleges and universities do indeed experience a heavy loss of students over the freshman and sophomore years, particularly in the first year, and thus, in a sense, have a large number of "noncollege" students in their student bodies. But four-year colleges do not attempt to provide special training or short-term alternatives for those that are early eliminated or identified as marginal. The colleges remain oriented toward the four-year program and the four-year student, and the first year of study takes its meaning from its part in a baccalaureate effort. For the two-year junior college, however, what happens to students in the thirteenth year is largely the heart of the matter. The fate of most students at that point cannot be ignored, and their destiny in fact is termination within several semesters.

The central point can be restated as follows: the basic problem of the junior college is the processing of the student who falls between the transfer and terminal groups. Students with transfer intentions for the most part do not transfer, but neither do they complete terminal curricula. Most terminate their education while in the college but do so as dropouts while pursuing transfer work. In this way, the modal student does not fall clearly into the transfer or terminal category, and the administration of curriculum and instruction is centrally concerned with the processing of this in-between type. This is an aspect of the junior college not shown in output categories, nor is it revealed in debate over whether the public junior college is primarily a transfer or a terminal training agency. The student who filters out of education while in the junior college appears to be very much what such a college is about.

The battle of the production line in the junior college is to hold on to a good share, if not all, of these students long enough to train them for an occupation or to add to their general education. This, however, the San Jose Junior College was largely not able to do by the end of its first four years, as indicated by the small numbers of graduates and terminally trained students. In this it is not unique, as shown by comparative data reported in this chapter. In short, the public junior college tends to be a classification and distribution center from which large numbers of students leave education after a relatively short stay.

CHAPTER 3

The Adaptation to Task

The preceding chapters described major conditions confronted by a new junior college: location in a public school administrative setting and a state admission policy of an open door to all comers. In this chapter we look directly at the structure and personnel of the organization. Effects of the control system and the unselected student body can be seen in many aspects of the college's development and operation. Patterns of organization changed to accommodate student pressures; an administrative staff was recruited that reflected district control and the nature of the student body; the teaching staff was similarly shaped. These features of the college reflect and depict its character.

THE EVOLUTION OF FORMAL PATTERNS

It was earlier shown that self-selected students appeared in greater numbers than anticipated by the college and with interests that changed the balance of programs from that which was planned. This situation in itself could be expected to unsettle whatever arrangements of personnel had existed initially. Then, too, the establishing of appropriate formal machinery was complicated by an overworking of personnel, which was occasioned by rapid expansion and district economy. Also contributing to structural growing pains, as will be seen, was the common organizational need of moving through stages of development according to changes in the importance of different tasks.

The initial formal structure of the college in the fall of 1953 was relatively simple. There were three senior administrators, a director, and two division chiefs. The division heads were designated as deans, one heading a division of technical and industrial education and the other a division of student services. The T. and I. (technical and industrial) dean was assisted by a part-time coordinator and the student services dean, by a full-time associate dean. These were the only administrative units and positions formally designated at the outset. Notably absent were divisions of instruction in fields other than technical and industrial education. Changes in this embryonic structure can be shown by describing the fate of these two initial divisions and one that later emerged.

The Relegation of T. and I.

The division of technical and industrial education came to the college as an organized unit that previously constituted a vocational evening high school under the aegis of the adult education department of the district. Its dean described the change-over in the summer of 1953: "On June 30, we were the Leland Vocational Evening High School and on July 1, we were the San Jose Junior College." The T. and I. administrators put on a summer session in 1953 that operationally was the entire college at the time. No other units or programs were similarly brought in from other schools, and this vocational group was early ahead in organization.

Promising for the welfare of T. and I. was the commitment of the district to a trade school conception of the college. If terminal vocational operations were to be highlighted, the T.

and I. division would be an important, if not the primary, unit of the college. No comparable units were established at the time of origin. In its organization of programs, the college spoke of a division of business education and a division of general education, but in personnel assignment these were largely paper divisions. Being the sole instructional division, there was ample reason for the technical and industrial division to expect an important role in the day work of the college. In addition, it was given jurisdiction over the entire evening program, which was to be largely vocational. This was no new effort for the T. and I. administrators, since they had previously been responsible for a similar evening program. They concentrated on the problem of reorienting their thinking and procedure to handle effectively their new daytime role.

The interests of the student body did not allow a build-up of an important vocational operation during the day, however, and the transformation early encountered by the college sharply downgraded the possible role of this division. Table 12 shows the relative importance of its work in terms of student enrollment. One-fifth of the student body was enrolled in T. and I. curricula during the first year. For a short time, this low percentage, along with the students' avoidance of other terminal offerings in business and general education, could be seen as a temporary phenomenon. Despite the example in other junior colleges of the fact that terminal work tends to be subordinated, it could be hoped that more attractive terminal courses and a change in students' perception of terminal curricula would materially strengthen this operation. The even lower percentages of the succeeding years, however, spelled a subsidiary place. With enrollment approximating 10 per cent of the day student body in the fourth year, the T. and I. operation was hardly in evidence in the day work of the college. The old-line shop classes (e.g., carpentry) had grown little—108 students in the fall semester of the fourth year compared to 71 in the opening semester—

Table 12
Enrollment in Technical and Industrial Majors,
San Jose Junior College,
1953–1954 to 1956–1957

Year and semester	Day enrollment*		
	All majors	T. and I. major	
		Number	Per cent
First year (1953–1954):			
Fall	539	108	20
Spring	625	129	21
Second year (1954–1955):			
Fall	1,376	257	19
Spring	1,523	251	16
Third year (1955–1956):			
Fall	1,788	236	13
Spring	1,800	222	12
Fourth year (1956–1957):			
Fall	2,133	244	11
Spring	1,847	194	10

* Day enrollment at opening of semester.
SOURCE: San Jose Junior College, Division of Student Services.

and only a sizable enrollment increase in terminal electronics work (from 37 students in the first year to 136 in the fourth) held the day work of the division to even a 10 per cent level of importance.

Table 13 indicates what happened in the growth of courses. About one-third of the college's courses were in technical and industrial subjects the first year. Between the first and fourth years, more than two hundred courses were added; nearly all of these were in the college's general category which included all academic subjects. This made technical courses 15 per cent of

Table 13

Distribution of Courses, First and Fourth Years, San Jose Junior College

Type of course*	Year				Increase in number of courses	
	1953–1954		1956–1957			
	Number†	Per cent	Number	Per cent	Number	Per cent
Technical and industrial	65	31	64	15	−1	−2
Business	36	17	45	11	9	25
General	107	52	310	74	203	190
Total	208	100	419	100	211	101

* According to the three major categories used by San Jose Junior College in 1953–1954 and 1956–1957.

† Semester-length courses, separately numbered in the college catalogue.

SOURCES: *San Jose Junior College Announcements for 1953–1954*, San Jose Unified School District, San Jose, 1953, and *San Jose Junior College Bulletin, 1956–1957*, San Jose Unified School District, San Jose, 1956.

the total in the fourth year. The proliferation of courses after the first year clearly took place in nonvocational subjects.

Meanwhile, the college's evening or extended-day program prospered, experiencing a boom comparable in magnitude to that of the regular day college. As seen in Table 14, the enrollment of part-time evening students was never less than approximately half of all enrollment, and generally throughout the four-year period, it surpassed the number of full-time day students. This evening operation was largely composed of technical and industrial classes; in the spring semester of the third year, for example, seventy-three of eighty-six classes, or 85 per cent, were in T. and I. subjects. In short, the technical and industrial offerings of the

Table 14
Day and Evening Enrollment,*
San Jose Junior College,
1953–1954 to 1956–1957

Year and semester	Combined enrollment of day and evening	Day enrollment		Evening enrollment	
		Number	Per cent	Number	Per cent
First year (1953–1954):					
Fall	1,424	505	36	919	64
Spring	1,643	585	36	1,058	64
Second year (1954–1955):					
Fall	2,481	1,284	52	1,197	48
Spring	2,707	1,384	51	1,323	49
Third year (1955–1956):					
Fall	3,383	1,689	50	1,694	50
Spring	3,438	1,676	49	1,762	51
Fourth year (1956–1957):					
Fall	4,326	1,941	45	2,385	55
Spring	4,746	1,900	40	2,846	60

* According to October and March enrollment reports. These figures are generally lower than opening enrollments because of dropouts.

SOURCE: San Jose Junior College, Division of Student Services.

college were found predominantly in the evening operation, and the evening work of the technical and industrial division dwarfed its day performance. At the end of the fourth year, this division enrolled approximately ten part-time evening students for every one full-time day student.

With increasing weakness during the day and increasing strength at night, this technical division became, in effect, the evening division of the college. Its administrators worked a night shift, an afternoon and evening schedule normal among adult education administrators, and its teaching force was part-time and evening rather than full-time day. This trend toward evening pulled the personnel of the division away from the regular day staff, reducing their participation in formal staff deliberations as well as greatly lessening their informal association with those who taught during the day.

At the end of four years, the division was not only in a peripheral position in respect to the central operations of the college, but was so "out of joint" in the formal structure that a change in its formal status was likely. Its day operation was smaller than most of the day departments that had been established and could logically, at best, be considered a department. At the same time, its evening work needed division-level administration and an appropriate title.[1] Such changes must not have been easy to anticipate at the outset, before the students transformed the work of the college.

Emergence of a Division of Instruction

When the first director of the college rendered his initial report to the San Jose Board of Education, while planning for the opening of the college, he recommended an administrative structure that "ultimately" would consist of five divisions. In addition to a division of student services, he proposed four instructional divisions: technical and industrial, business, general terminal, and college transfer.[2] At the time, however, the direc-

[1] At the beginning of the fifth year, the dean of the division was held responsible to the director of the college "in all matters relating to the Extended Day Program" and the summer session "currently"—and these alone. *San Jose Junior College Faculty Handbook,* San Jose Unified School District, San Jose, September, 1957, p. 12.

[2] San Jose Unified School District, Minutes of the Board of Education, Dec. 18, 1952.

tor was willing, "for practical purposes of administration, as well as for reasons of sensible economy," to see these divisions "grouped together until such time as future enrollment may justify their ultimate separation." [3] Although the administration of the several divisions would finally need to be full-time, the director asked that during the planning stage he be provided with part-time administrative assistance for the T. and I. and student services divisions, together with part-time assistance from a teacher in business education. The board assigned three persons as requested, and an administrative nucleus was started. When the college opened six months later, the two half-time administrators became deans of their divisions; this was the extent to which personnel units were formally separated at the outset. At the end of four years, the recommended structure of four instructional divisions was nowhere in sight; in its place had emerged a general division of instruction that embraced terminal and transfer education and in which business education and technical training were placed as departments. This emergent structure was related to the pressure of clientele and to the managing of the latent terminal student.

The unanticipated size and interest of the college's student body produced an almost intolerable situation in the early administration of instruction. At the time the college opened, the students' interest in transfer work required rapid assembly of academic curricula, and the later expansion in enrollment of students with similar interest meant large units organized around academic subjects. Yet, formally, there was little preparation, and no one was directly assigned to administer instruction in other than technical and industrial education. To help the situation, the college commissioned a teacher as an instructional head and instructed the teaching staff to take curriculum problems to him. In the middle of the first year, this teacher was formally appointed dean of instruction by the board of educa-

[3] *Ibid.*

tion,[4] only to resign and leave the district for another position at the end of the year. During the second and third years, instructional authority was shared by the director, the dean and associate dean of student services, the dean of T. and I., and a large curriculum committee of teachers. Lines of authority were ambiguous, most teachers being outside the existing structure of divisions. It was not until the fourth year that a dean of instruction with broad responsibilities was hired and that a division of instruction began to take formal shape.

The confusion in instructional administration, wrought by the size and interest of the student body, was deepened by the turnover and shortage of administrators. The first director of the college shouldered many instructional responsibilities, particularly during the second year, after the original dean of instruction had resigned and the director himself had become convinced that he should step down from the top position. His successor-to-be was appointed acting assistant director in the second year, and spent much of the third year taking hold of the college. The first director resigned at the end of the second year and left the district. This meant that the difficulties caused by the loss of the first dean of instruction were compounded in the second and third years by succession in the directorship. This helped to postpone a formalization of the changes that were taking place in the lower echelons of the staff.

For, while the small, top administrative group was in flux, an organizational build-up was taking place from below, with departments emerging in academic disciplines. Where the college had opened with a full-time teaching force of only eleven, in the fourth year the cluster of subjects denoted as social science (economics, geography, history, political science, sociology) in itself had nine instructors. By the third year, instructional personnel were approximately grouped in fifteen departments, some

[4] San Jose Unified School District, Minutes of the Board of Education, Jan. 7, 1954.

Table 15
Instructional Departments of San Jose Junior College, 1955–1956

Department	Total class enrollment	Number of courses	Number of sections	Average class size*
Social Science	1,583	16	31	51
English and Journalism	1,533	15	46	33
Business	1,459	32	45	32
Physical Education	1,206	8	48	25
Science	972	17	34	29
Psychology, Philosophy, Education	928	5	18	52
Mathematics	684	11	27	25
Drama and Speech	381	7	14	27
Art	332	14	15	22
Technical and Industrial	275	18	26	11
Industrial Arts	237	7	12	20
Music	236	10	10	24
Hygiene	227	1	8	28
Foreign Languages	81	5	5	16
Home Economics	49	4	4	12
Total	10,183	170	343	30

* Enrollment divided by number of sections.

SOURCE: San Jose Junior College, Division of Student Services, "San Jose Junior College" (mimeographed report on enrollment and student characteristics), Sept. 21, 1956.

of which were large operations. The departments as of that time are listed in Table 15; as can be seen, four departments exceeded one thousand students in class enrollment and seven exceeded five hundred students. Eight of the departments were giving ten or more courses, with an even larger number of sections, and two departments showed an average class size of more than fifty.

The technical and industrial division, already referred to on occasion as a department, was well down among the smaller operations of day instruction, exceeded even by the art department. The departments were administered by full-time teachers serving additionally as department chairmen.

None of these departments except the technical and industrial was engaged in transfer or terminal work alone but embraced both. For example, the large business department was by no means a terminal unit, although it had two-year programs in office work, accounting, and selling. Nearly 70 per cent of its majors, 347 of 500 students, were registered as transfer students. The department structures, organized around subjects, did not distinguish between terminal and transfer operations in the way that terminal and transfer departments would. It made the most sense and served the most faculty interests to have subject-field nuclei. Similarly, as division-level administration began to crystallize in a relatively permanent form in the fourth year, it was not realistic that a college transfer division should be clearly demarcated from terminal divisions, in the type of structure originally thought feasible. This arrangement would have split subject fields, assigning some teachers and courses in business, for example, to one division and some to another. Such a clear demarcation of the transfer and the terminal student would have also rendered the managing of the latent terminal student more difficult. He would have to be reassigned to a second division and pick up with different courses and perhaps different instructors. In addition, the terminal segments in themselves never became sufficiently large to be economically constituted as separate divisions. The drift was in the other direction with the technical program moving from separate division to department status. The emerging division and department structure reflected the transfer orientation of the students and the college's need to smooth the movement of students across the transfer-terminal line. From an initial organization of instruction that attempted to emphasize a terminal field, the college evolved a structure that embraced a wide gamut of curricula in one comprehensive division. In this major unit, subject areas found a place at a department level and without regard to differences between two-year and four-year students.

Student Services

Provided at the outset with divisional stature and staffed with two deans, the unit responsible for student services occupied a central position in the college. The dean and associate dean of this division were one-half of the full-time administrative staff during the first three years, and the director and the vocational dean were the other half. This division was responsible for nearly all activities that touched the student outside the classroom—registration, counseling, veterans' affairs, placement, extracurricular programs—and also entered into instruction through the counseling and orientation classes. In addition, the "mechanics of course organization" and "graduation requirements" were assigned to the division.[5] The division was well placed in the physical plant of the college, occupying most of the space available in the administration building. Instructional personnel, in contrast, were scattered and for the most part had little office space outside the classroom.

The reasons for the central place of this division's administrative staff were many. A junior college has normally a stronger urge toward guidance and counseling activities than most colleges, because the routing and rerouting of students is an important part of operations. The student services deans were also thrust into administrative prominence by the occurrences that weakened the other segments of administration; that is, the relegation of T. and I. to the evening, the turnover in the directorship, and the absence of appropriate instructional organization. In the work rush of the early years, these features caused teachers

[5] *Ibid.*, Dec. 18, 1952.

to turn to whoever was available and informed. The deans of student services provided much of the college's administrative continuity and in the process of filling breaches, assumed much instructional authority.

Important in the early upgrading of student services, however, were the demands of early organization. Much attention needed to be given in the beginning to work done *on* the college rather than to work done *by* it. The machinery of work had to be established in some minimal form, and in a new school many of the unavoidable problems of mechanics center on the processing and handling of students. Students need to be admitted, registered, and placed on an instructional track; hence, procedures were immediately needed for admission, registration, and assignment to curricula and classes. The early concerns of the first director reflected the importance of housekeeping matters. After proposing the general outline of an administrative structure to the board of education in December, 1952, the director turned to "major problems yet to be considered." First among these was "the probable size and distribution of student enrollments"; second, "housing and plant"; third, "a listing and organization of the actual courses to be offered"; and fourth, "the selection and assignment of teaching personnel," the latter to be deferred until progress in "specific operational detail" was more complete.[6] Even after the doors of the college opened, instruction mattered little at first compared to the general problem of establishing minimal order in a potentially chaotic situation. The gearing of the organizational machinery, so that instruction and other activities might later take place effectively, fell largely within the broad province of the division of student services. In this way, the importance of mechanics in the earliest, most undeveloped stage of organization enhanced the role of this unit.

It was unlikely that this role would remain quite so central, however, because as the organization as a whole turned to pro-

[6] *Ibid.*

duction, the "line" structure of the college would tend to form around instruction. It could be expected that student services, in turn, would tend toward the "staff" status of an auxiliary service. The major build-up of organization did, in fact, take place around instructional departments. In the fourth year, more than three-fourths of the professional personnel of the college were to be found in the newly formed division of instruction. As mentioned previously, large departments within this division alone had a staff of nine or ten. In contrast, the division of student services had added to its original staff a registrar who was half-time in the third year and full-time in the fourth. The division had no full-time counselors, using teachers part-time. With this arrangement the division's share of professional personnel approximated 10 per cent. Its direct authority, like that of dean of students and registrar units elsewhere in college administration, was over a clerical staff and certain aspects of student participation, but hardly constituted direct command over instructors on important matters. The decisive change in authority was the appointment of a dean of instruction in the fourth year; with the filling of this post, a clearer distinction emerged between matters of instruction and matters of student service. As the new dean took hold, instructional responsibility in the college naturally began to center in his office. His position was formally second only to the director in breadth and level of authority. His duties extended to all key matters of curriculum and instruction. He participated in the selection of teachers, along with the director of the college and the administrative staff of central headquarters. In such matters, student services had little influence.

To summarize the divisional changes: It was initially planned that a vocational division would have a central role in the work of the college. But because of student preferences, this division was soon relegated to a subsidiary position. The second of two original divisions, one for student services, remained strong through the first several years but by the fourth year showed signs of assuming the place of an auxiliary staff division. This change was related to a shift in attention from mechanics to instruction and to the tendency in college organization for instructional divisions and departments to occupy the center of the stage. Both changes were largely undesired by the district authorities and also by the college authorities. Only reluctantly was the downgrading of the terminal technical operation accepted; and an attempt was made, with somewhat more success, to hold student services to a status equal to instruction. The assuming of central place by a new academic division was forced on the college largely by trends in enrollment, task importance, and personnel assignment. That the organization of the college in its fourth year centered on a complex of academic departments appears to be a clear indication of the influence of students. The reorganization of instructional authority in the fourth year through the appointment of a dean of instruction with broad powers was, in effect, an admission that the college was not to be a technical institute.

The formal structure of the college which existed at the end of four years had clearly been thrashed out the hard way. In major respects, the structure formalized arrangements of work and personnel which were caused by unplanned and uncontrolled developments. This drift in formal structure was magnified by turnover and understaffing in administrative positions. Under the best conditions, however, some structural drift would have occurred. Formal changes cannot be fully anticipated, and when organizational trends run counter to original intentions, much unguided evolution is likely. The type of change that occurred in San Jose Junior College may well be more frequent among organizations than is indicated by the common conception that formal structure is a planned arrangement. Formal schemes frequently record and further regularize patterns of action that have become customary in nonformal ways.[7] The evolution occurring in the college's first four years seems to be clearly a case in point of this sociological view, for the changing patterns of organization were more a formalization of what had come about than an early anticipation of what was to occur.

ADMINISTRATIVE ORIENTATION

One matter in which the students of the college had no direct influence was the selection of administrative personnel. In this, district control was decisive. The district, it will be recalled, wanted for one thing a vocationally oriented college. Toward this end, the central staff of the district manned the new college with administrators versed in vocational education and possessing skill and experience in handling a trade school student body. The dean of technical and industrial education, for example, was an experienced vocational educator, former head of an evening vocational school. The associate dean of student services came to the college from a position in the San Jose Technical High School. The first director of the college had been the principal of a "tough" junior high school in the district, with proven ability in dealing with the type of student likely to enter a trade training establishment. This was also true for the second director, whose experience as assistant principal in the same junior high was followed by a principalship in a San Jose senior high school. The second director also had a personal interest in vocational education, and soon after his appointment, took an active part in building an electronics program. The dean of student services came from the principalship of a small high school that had con-

[7] For a general statement of this sociological view, see Philip Selznick, *Leadership in Administration*, Row, Peterson & Company, Evanston, Ill., 1957, p. 12.

tinuation students[8] and other special students. Even the dean of instruction, appointed in the fourth year, had taken early administrative training in vocational education; and although coming to the college from a position of elementary supervisor in district headquarters, he served in the year preceding his appointment as secretary to the Study Committee for Industrial Education, the group embroiled in the Technical High School controversy. The administrative staff, although not unacquainted with academic work, was clearly better prepared for a vocationally oriented enterprise.

As a second common characteristic, all administrators of the college came from positions *within* the district. This was not accidental. Internal selection was directly related to integrated management of the district. Along with the unified-district point of view described in Chapter 1 went an expectation on the part of district officials that a demonstrated attachment to the district should be a prime requirement in considering appointments to strategic field positions. It is important in managing a unified district that field administrators do not go their separate ways, pulling apart from other units and particularly from headquarters control. A junior college in a unified district is a special concern on this account, because some persons are bound to be employed in the college who will feel that their school ought to be treated differently from elementary and secondary schools. Besides, the chief administrator of a college has a post that, in time, can come to rival that of the superintendent in prestige and influence. In implementing its unified point of view, the San Jose district selected persons who had come up through the parent organization and who, for the most part, had assimi-

[8] Continuation students are students that have dropped out of school after passing the compulsory attendance age (sixteen) but have not completed high school. They are expected to attend school four hours a week until they reach eighteen or complete high school.

lated its philosophy and learned to accept its authority. The district did not recruit from outside its own personnel.

In this connection it should be mentioned that the district maintained authority over many matters. Chapter 1 indicated a general budgetary control and also suggested that parts of the college were under dual authority, for example, the district's director of vocational education was given a strong voice in the administering of the college's vocational work. Besides, in the central matter of selecting teachers, district-headquarters personnel took a part. Applicants were interviewed by the assistant superintendent in charge of instruction or by the deputy superintendent, in addition to being seen by the director of the college and his immediate associates. Headquarters agreement had to be obtained on appointees, and their beginning salary was largely determined by the deputy superintendent. Then, too, the college's course offerings had to be approved by the district, so that even in the determination of the educational program, administrators outside the college had a voice. The staff members of the college, in answering a questionnaire item, described this voice as often being the most powerful one of all. To the question, "Who would you say has the most powerful voice on your campus in determining the educational program of your college?" the most frequent response (32 per cent) was the superintendent of schools. Another 9 per cent nominated the board of education, making a total of 41 per cent who specified an authority external to the college itself. About 17 per cent said the junior college president; 19 per cent, the faculty as a whole; 11 per cent, a dean or the college administrators together; and 8 per cent, heads of departments. Clearly district authority is felt, and possibly exaggerated, by the staff even in an area where authority in colleges normally resides with the faculty. With district influence pervasive, it was probably necessary that administrators for the college be selected that were trustworthy from the district's point of view and habituated to its modes of operation. Appointment of district men would contribute to a mutual understanding and, as promotion from within the system, would also aid morale within the administrative corps of the district.

Selection on the grounds of district loyalty deemphasized such criteria as experience and proven ability in junior college administration. The way to get the best man for the job, of course, in the sense of junior college administration per se, is to canvass the field. The district's concern with unified management made loyalty primary over expertise.[9] Access to junior college administrative posts was defined to be from within the immediate school system.

It can also be seen that the college's administrators possessed a third common characteristic, namely, an administrative background predominantly, if not entirely, in the elementary or secondary school. All the college's officials gained their general administrative outlook, formed habits of work, and learned procedure in such units, principally in junior and senior high schools. None had college administrative experience. With such uniformity of background, the know-how brought to bear in the administration of the college had to be that of the public schools and not that of four-year colleges or universities.

It is instructive to seek the possible influence of these aspects of administrative background. Clearly the vocational background of the administrators did not orient the college but was largely submerged by the persistently antivocational choices of the students. In their attitudes, however, the administrators as a whole stuck by their vocational guns. This is reflected in questionnaire responses. Seven out of ten administrators agreed with a questionnaire item that "the main emphasis in the junior col-

[9] For a general discussion of the need for loyalty versus the need for expertise in organizations, see Alvin W. Gouldner, "Cosmopolitans and Locals: Toward an Analysis of Latent Social Roles, II," *Administrative Science Quarterly*, vol. 2, no. 4, pp. 463–467, March, 1958.

lege should be on vocational education," while only 9 per cent of the teachers of academic subjects and 30 per cent of the teachers of applied subjects (vocational and business) so agreed. This item is shown as the first question in Table 16. This table reports fifteen questions out of forty analyzed for differences in attitude within the staff; these items all show a difference of more than 20 per cent between the administrators and the academic teachers of the college and are arranged in descending order of size of difference. The question of vocational education as the main emphasis of the junior college produced the greatest disagreement. An interest in vocational work on the part of the administrators is also reflected in other items in this table. In question 3, the administrators uniformly disagreed with the statement that "programs such as cosmetology should have no place in the junior college curriculum," while nearly half (45 per cent) of the academic teachers agreed with the statement. Here, as in most of the other questions, it may be noted that the teachers of applied subjects came much closer to the view of the administrators than to the view of the academic teachers. Typically (other than in question 4) the administrators had the most "applied" view, the vocational and business teachers had an applied view to lesser degree, and the academic teachers had the least applied view.

Question 4 shows only four out of ten administrators accepting the idea that "the junior college should not do for industry what industry can do for itself," while the academic teachers overwhelmingly (82 per cent) agree with this. Question 6 can also be read for its vocational or applied meaning; if Americans ought to be able to have some higher education regardless of interest in traditional academic subjects, then they apparently should be allowed into college on the basis of interest in nonacademic or applied subjects. Eighty per cent of the administrators and also 80 per cent of the teachers of applied subjects agreed with the question, but only less than half (44 per cent) of the academic teachers agreed. In question 9, administrators were all

Table 16

Differences in the Point of View of Administrators and Teachers, San Jose Junior College (In per cent)

Question response	College position				
	Adminis-trator (*N* = 10)		"Academic teacher" (*N* = 45)	"Applied teacher"* (*N* = 31)	Total college (*N* = 86)
Agree that:					
(1) the main emphasis in the junior college should be on vocational education.	70	(61)†	9	30	23
(2) the community should have a considerable voice in determining the curriculum of the public junior college.	100	(56)	44	68	59
(3) programs such as cosmetology should have no place in the junior college curriculum.	0	(45)	45	3	25
(4) the junior college should not do for industry what industry can do for itself.	40	(42)	82	33	60
(5) four-year colleges and universities play too great a role in determining junior college programs.	50	(37)	13	40	27
(6) all Americans ought to be able to have some higher education regardless of whether they have any interest in the subjects that traditionally comprise the academic curriculum of the four-year college or university.	80	(36)	44	80	61
(7) in comparison with the four-year college, the junior college is at a disadvantage in providing opportunities for a well-rounded program of social activities for its students.	30	(32)	62	40	51
(8) the junior college is usually closer to the needs of the community than is the four-year college or university.	100	(31)	69	90	80

Table 16 (*Continued*)

Question response	College position			
	Administrator (N = 10)	"Academic teacher" (N = 45)	"Applied teacher"* (N = 31)	Total college (N = 86)
(9) there should be two distinct kinds of junior colleges—one to offer traditional lower-division college work, the other to offer semiprofessional and vocational training.	0 (31)	31	6	19
(10) the administration of a junior college is more likely to give recognition to a good teacher than is a four-year college or university.	60 (29)	31	45	39
(11) scholastic entrance requirements for junior colleges are too low for the most part.	20 (27)	47	45	43
(12) all Americans ought to be able to have some higher education regardless of whether they have taken the proper courses in secondary school to prepare them for higher education.	90 (26)	64	87	76
(13) the junior college is too oriented to "life adjustment" education.	0 (24)	24	10	16
(14) the junior college should offer a flexible program which can be adjusted to the needs of society, unhampered by conventional notions of what constitutes higher education.	90 (23)	67	74	72
(15) faculty relationships at the junior college are likely to be more congenial than faculty relationships at the four-year college or university.	80 (20)	60	74	67

* "Applied teachers" means teachers of vocational and business subjects. All other teachers were classified as "academic."

† Difference between administrators and academic teachers.

SOURCE: Junior college teacher questionnaire; see Appendix 1.

against separating vocational education from lower-division college work, while nearly a third (31 per cent) of the academic teachers agreed with the idea of two distinct kinds of junior colleges. These differences suggest that the administrators of the college did indeed "think vocationally," a tendency toward which they would be disposed by background and also by the vocational pressure from district headquarters.

The role of the second background factor, the earlier experience of the administrators in the same district, had a more tenuous impact on the college and in administrative attitudes. For several administrators, a long history of close official and personal relationships with other district administrators helped to keep them sympathetic to problems and policies of the district. Mutual understanding was promoted. For others, this was not the case, with the needs of junior college administration causing a rapid attenuation of district commitment. The first director of the college tended to pull away from the district in the process of contending with the college's evolution toward transfer work. Close to the emerging trends, the director came to feel that the district's original purpose and its level of financing were unrealistic. Other administrators similarly strained against the headquarters point of view. In this they were encouraged by teachers and students and by their own gradually forming conception of what was good for the college.

One questionnaire item (not shown in Table 16) bore on this matter, and the San Jose responses to it sharply reflected the desire of the administrators, as well as the teachers, to be outside a unified district. To the proposition that "a junior college should be administratively autonomous, having its own Board of Trustees," 94 per cent of the college's staff assented. All major subdivisions of the staff agreed, with the administrators "overwhelmingly" [10] agreeing. It would appear that devotion to the

[10] This term is used instead of a number to protect the anonymity of individual responses on a relatively sensitive issue. It means 70 per cent or more.

college had come to take precedence over loyalty to the district. At the same time, however, an attitude may be one thing and action another. The administrators were frequently constrained to behave in ways that teachers saw as unduly favoring the district. Here background could hardly be disentangled in analysis from official direction. The administrators had always, in part, to be an arm of the district. Like most men of middle management, they were caught between the differing expectations of those above and below them. On any major bone of contention, it can be said, the college administrators felt impelled to heed district desires. As administrators, they did not possess tenure and were removable on district order. The college officials had to live with district authority. For this their district background had provided a preparation and perhaps a tolerance not likely to be possessed by men recruited from the outside.

The aspect of administrative background that most clearly fitted the new setting was that of public school training and outlook. Earlier administrative experience in the public schools related well to the nature of the college's student body and to many of the rules and expectations of district administration. For example, with public school experience, the administrators of the college would not be so likely to find the ability level of the student body unnaturally low. It was similar to what they had known in the past, whereas administrators with a collegiate background would more likely see it as unusual, possibly shocking. The heterogeneity of the student body was similarly familiar to those prepared by public school work. Also, the application of certain district procedures to this new unit would not seem out of line, despite its college label, where administrators from a different background might find them questionable. Why should junior college teachers be placed on a single salary schedule together with elementary and high school teachers? One salary schedule for all teachers is a normal procedure in public school administration, and men who had been principals of junior and senior high schools would not be so likely to challenge its applicability to the junior college as would others without this experience. Men with a background in college administration might well think of college teaching as sufficiently different from elementary and secondary work to require a separate system of statuses and pay. As a final example, maintaining official class records for the purpose of reporting attendance to the state is a well-known standard operating procedure for those with public school experience. In short, such a background would be appropriate for college administrators that faced a public school type of clientele and operated within a public school control system.

Here again questionnaire results give some clues to the sympathy of the administrators for public school procedure and outlook. Question 2 in Table 16 can be interpreted in this vein, because it is a public school doctrine, and not an ideology of colleges, that "the community should have considerable voice in determining the curriculum" of a school, in this case "of the public junior college." The administrators agreed with this completely, but of the academic teachers, only 44 per cent agreed. Out of forty questions this was the item of second-largest disagreement between the two groups. Question 5 can be similarly interpreted; the view that "four-year colleges and universities play too great a role in determining junior college program[s]" can be taken as a public school position. Only 13 per cent of the academic teachers thought this correct, but half of the administrators did. In all fifteen questions of Table 16, the administrators appear to take a stand favoring the public school: as examples, all administrators agreed that "the junior college is usually closer to the needs of the community than is the four-year college or university" (question 8), and nine out of ten agreed that "all Americans ought to be able to have some higher education regardless of whether they have taken the proper courses in secondary school."

As a concluding point, the district selection of "district men" to administer the college is a clear example of what might generally be known as *restraint by recruitment*.[11] The district attempted to secure conformity to district and public school norms through selection of men with appropriate backgrounds. The uniformity of the backgrounds would also help to produce homogeneity of outlook. These restraints were not fully controlling and deviation from the desired norms did occur. But the general effect of the district's form of recruitment was to give the administration of the college a public school cast and to restrain somewhat the tendency for the college to go its own way.

THE COLLEGE INSTRUCTOR

Even in a type of college strongly interested in counseling, guidance, and other nonteaching activities, teaching does not lose its traditionally central place. As seen earlier in this chapter, the professional staff of San Jose Junior College expanded and became organized principally around instruction, as would normally be expected. Of interest here are the expectations brought to bear on the instructional position by the district authorities and the college administration. The available evidence indicates a tendency to model that position after the high school.

One source of information on this matter is the college's *Faculty Handbook*, a document used in the orientation of new

[11] Richard Hofstadter has suggested that restraint by recruitment is the primary instrument of control in colleges. He noted the close religious conformity exacted of teachers in their appointment to college staffs in the eighteenth century. See Richard Hofstadter and Walter P. Metzger, *The Development of Academic Freedom in the United States*, Columbia University Press, New York, 1955, pp. 155–156. Restraint by recruitment is widely used in organizations that want to maintain or build an "outlook." Then a recruit needs to have "proper" values as well as technical competence.

faculty members. The handbook opens with the statement that it was prepared for "the certificated personnel" of the college, an expression foreign to college administration but common to the public schools where teaching certificates are needed. Subsequently, the handbook specifies what is expected of the instructor in relation to the administration of the college and the district. The following official rules were excerpted because they bear on important aspects of teaching (for example, the number of hours in the classroom each week) or because they illustrate the tone of lesser matters of work (e.g., chaperoning student activities):

On teaching load:

> The normal load for lecture subjects is 18 hours per week; for laboratory, physical education, and most shop courses, 24 hours; and for Technical-Industrial shops, 30 hours.

On salary:

> Salaries of all full-time certificated employees of the San Jose Unified School District are determined on the basis of their placement on a single salary schedule. Placement is based on training, years of experience and professional growth. . . . Part-time instructors in the Extended Day Program are paid an hourly rate designated by the Board of Education for Adult Education teachers.

On credential requirements:

> Instructors must hold a General Secondary Credential, Junior College Credential, or Special Secondary Credential. Instructors holding the latter two types have the period of probationary status in which to qualify for the General Secondary Credential, which District policy requires for tenure.

On tenure:

> Instructors who are accepted for the fourth year of employment in the San Jose Unified School District pass from probationary to tenure status.

On retirement:

All credentialed teachers by law are members of the California State Teachers' Retirement system, and salary deductions for payment into the retirement fund are mandatory.

On the keeping of class records:

The Class Record is the official document for all attendance accounting, and for this reason must be kept accurately up to date.

On chaperoning and officiating:

It is the policy of the Board of Education to consider both teaching and extra curricular assignments of the schools as part of the teaching load of the school.

Appointment of chaperons is made: (1) by Assistant Dean of Student Services for athletic events (2) by Dean of Student Services for social events (3) by club advisor for club affairs.

On faculty meetings:

When faculty meetings are called, each instructor is expected to attend.

On instructor rating:

Instructors will be rated annually in the spring during the first three years of their service in the District.

On absence of the instructor:

If ill or unable to attend, the instructor in the Day Program is requested to notify the Dean of Instruction as early as possible. A phone call for this purpose should be made to the Dean's home not later than 7 A.M. of the day of absence.

Provision for a substitute will normally be made on a day-to-day basis, so the College must be notified for each succeeding day of the absence. . . . Each scheduled class must be met.

On assembly hours and schedule:

Each Tuesday during the Day schedule, the 10:30 hour is kept free for student assemblies and activities.

On teacher institute days:

> Teacher institute days are spaced throughout the year as afternoon or evening meetings and instructors are informed when these institute meetings occur.

Virtually without exception these rules stem from a public school context and take their meaning from a public school orientation. The typical instructional load is eighteen hours a week in the classroom, with three to five course preparations (the latter is not specified above). This work load is heavy by college standards, for example, six to nine hours commonly at the University of California, twelve hours at the California state colleges; but the work load is light in the district where it is compared to the twenty-five-hour assignment of the high school teacher and thirty-hour assignments of the elementary school. When the faculty of the college seeks a lighter teaching load, it is confronted by this public school frame of reference. In addition, extracurricular tasks are defined as part of the normal work load and "assignments" made. One interviewed teacher compared this situation with what he had experienced while teaching in San Jose State College, as follows: "At State, students ask a man to be a chaperone and he is free to decline. At the Junior College, such extracurricular tasks are assigned to teachers." Then, as noted earlier, salary scale is arrived at through a schedule shared with elementary and high school personnel. With this, and in contrast with other forms of college organization, the instructors do not have professorial title and rank.[12] Also seen in the quotations above is an explicit definition of the teacher as employee, for example, the reference to "certificated employees" of the district in the statement on salaries. Other items quoted

[12] Nonprofessorial status for teachers is common among junior colleges throughout the nation. Only about one-sixth of the junior colleges (public and private) of the country designate their faculty members by the typical higher-education ranks. See *Higher Education,* U.S. Department of Health, Education, and Welfare, vol. 14, no. 7, p. 107, March, 1958.

Table 17
Source of Teaching Personnel,
San Jose Junior College,
1956–1957

Previous position or activity	Full-time teachers	
	Number	Per cent
High school	45	67
Four-year college or university	10	15
Student background only	9	13
Other junior colleges	2	3
Other than education	1	2
Total	67	100

SOURCE: San Jose Junior College files.

indicate that the college's teachers must have a public school credential, receive tenure in the district as a whole, must personally meet every scheduled class or arrange for a substitute teacher, and have available to them teacher institutes which they may attend in order to pick up "professional-growth" credit on the salary schedule. These rules are clearly part of a public school ethos, casting the instructional position in a high school mold, away from the styles of four-year colleges and universities.

As to teacher selection, a similar cast is given to the instructional role. The main recruitment base of the college is the public high school. As seen in Table 17, two out of three full-time teachers on the staff in 1956–1957 had come to the college from high school positions.[13] Ten instructors, or 15 per cent, came from a position in a senior college or university, and of these,

[13] Nationally, about 64 per cent of junior college teachers have had secondary school experience. See Leland L. Medsker, *The Junior College: Progress and Prospect,* McGraw-Hill Book Company, Inc., New York, 1960, chap. 7.

seven were from San Jose State College. Nine teachers, or 13 per cent, came without experience directly from college; five of these were graduates of the state college. All of these inexperienced teachers were, in effect, prepared for high school positicns because they came to the college with some form of secondary credential. The number of teachers from high school increased through time, and was greatest in the fourth year when twelve of fifteen new teachers, or 80 per cent, were from this source. High school background becomes even more prominent when administrators and part-time vocational instructors are considered. All administrators save one came directly from junior or senior high schools, and the T. and I. instructors were from, and shared with, the local technical high school. Altogether, three out of four members of the professional staff had their previous position in secondary education.

The teachers with public school background, however, were not recruited predominantly from the San Jose district. Twenty-nine of the forty-five teachers with high school roots (64 per cent) were from other districts; and of the teachers with such a background, hired in the third and fourth years, nearly four out of five were from outside the immediate system. This out-of-district background contrasts sharply with the district background of the entire administrative staff. The administrators, it will be recalled, were selected as district dependables; filling new administrative posts from the district also had the advantage for morale of giving promotions to those with time in the system. As for teachers, however, relations among the administrators of the various district schools militated against heavy recruitment from the district. If the college had "raided" the staffs of the local high schools, it would have brought down on its head the antipathy of administrators not willing to surrender experienced teachers. On this ground alone it was appropriate to recruit teachers from the outside, even when local teachers were eager to take the position. In addition, the outside teachers did not have tenure in the district; hence they offered the administrative advantage of being subject to probationary trial before gaining permanency. Junior college vacancies were not "posted" within the district.

It is possible that the high school was the principal source of teachers because personnel were not available from other sources. This is plausible in view of the likelihood that many public school teachers will define junior college teaching as a desirable step upward, while persons experienced in or oriented toward the university or four-year college may think of it as a step downward, and therefore not make themselves available. But this was not the case; the college did not attempt to recruit heavily from the staffs of senior colleges or from the recent graduates and graduate students of the university. The reason was evident: administrators and teachers alike reported in interview that (1) work experience in the public schools contributes to success in junior college instruction and (2) the likelihood of difficult and unsuccessful adjustment in the teaching position is considerable when other sources are used. Those reporting this observation included teachers who, without the desired high school experience and after some difficulty, had been able to make the necessary adjustment. An analysis of the work history of teachers who had separated from the college tended to support this explanation, since it showed that eight out of ten teachers who had left the college had little or no public school experience. The experience of the college itself, as well as that of other junior colleges from which cues could have been taken, suggested the wisdom of building the instructional staff around public school teachers.

Another factor restraining recruitment from sources other than the public high school was the district requirement of a teaching credential, a rule indicative of the administrative definition of instructional work. As indicated in an above quotation from the college's *Faculty Handbook,* a teacher is expected to

Table 18

Type of Teaching Credential of San Jose Junior College Teachers, 1956–1957

Credential*	Teachers	
	Number	Per cent
General secondary	44	66
Special secondary or vocational	11	16
Junior college	4	6
Not reported or none	8	12
Total	67	100

* Some teachers held more than one credential but each person was counted only once. The general secondary was considered dominant over special credentials, when a teacher had both; one person tabulated under general secondary also had a junior college credential.

SOURCE: San Jose Junior College.

have some kind of public school credential at the time of employment and must secure a general secondary credential by his fourth year because the district requires it for tenure. Table 18 shows that two-thirds of the teachers possessed this particular license in the college's fourth year and that more than four out of five held some form of secondary credential. Only a few had a junior college credential alone. Among the teachers that had separated from the staff, an inappropriate credential had been judged a weakness by the college administration in several cases.

Requiring a general secondary credential for permanent employment in the college meant, of course, that *experienced* teachers had to come largely from a high school background. It also meant that the teachers of the college had taken the preprofessional training and had fulfilled the educational requirements normally exacted of high school teachers. As a corollary, the teachers were not prepared in the manner traditional to four-year colleges or universities—training devoted to subject matter to the exclusion of method—or specifically in junior college work.

The possession of a high school credential by the instructors had several advantages for district administration. The junior college teacher must have some form of certification to work in a unit legally defined as part of the state school system, and the general secondary credential is administratively more flexible than a credential limited to junior college teaching alone. The general license does not provide a symbol of difference between junior college and high school staffs, as a more specialized type would, and it smoothes the path for transfer of personnel between schools. If the district wished to transfer a high school teacher into the college or vice versa, for whatever reason, it would not be blocked by a difference in credential requirements. The junior college teacher is thus made more interchangeable with other district teachers; in the process he loses some measure of job control. Several years after its establishment, the college encountered a situation where a teacher was removed from a position elsewhere in the district and assigned to the college, against its own wishes, for the good of the district. This would not have been possible if a different credential had been required. The use of a common rather than a particular form of licensing is one way to enhance district maneuverability and control.

The college also selected teacher background in the form of level of education. Table 19 shows the highest academic degree held by full-time teachers. About 5 per cent had no degree, 31 per cent had a bachelor's degree, 60 per cent a master's, and 5 per cent (three teachers) a doctorate. The college had essentially a non-Ph.D. staff.[14] This aspect of background is related to se-

[14] Medsker's national sample indicates that this is a characteristic of junior college staffs generally. In his survey, 64 per cent of the teachers held an M.A., 7 per cent a Ph.D., and 3 per cent an Ed.D. About 19 per cent had a

Table 19

Educational Background of San Jose Junior College Teachers, 1956–1957

Highest college degree	Teachers	
	Number	Per cent
No degree	3	4 5
Bachelor	21	31.3
Master	40	59.7
Doctorate	3	4.5
Total	67	100.0

SOURCE: San Jose Junior College.

lection from the high school, and it also reflects a conception of the level of formal training appropriate for the staff. The college considers it desirable for a teacher to have proceeded in his own education as far as a master's degree, and this in a "subject-matter" discipline; past that point, however, lies the danger of the academician. The man with the Ph.D. is thought to be oriented toward the point of view of the university or the four-year liberal arts college, and he is thought of as likely to have the feeling that he should be teaching a parallel student body. The

bachelor's as their highest degree and 7 per cent no degree at all. Medsker, *op. cit.*, chap. 7. Another report shows the way the junior college, the state college, and the state university compare in California regarding faculty educational background. Holding a doctor's degree at time of appointment were 6 per cent of the junior college teachers, 43 per cent in the state colleges, and 80 per cent in the university; holding a bachelor's degree or no degree at time of appointment were 29 per cent in the junior colleges, 10 per cent in the state colleges, and 4 per cent in the university. *A Study of Faculty Demand and Supply in California Higher Education, 1957–1970,* The Liaison Committee of the Regents of the University of California and the California State Board of Education, Berkeley and Sacramento, 1958, pp. 28–36.

Ph.D. is regarded as concerned only with the better students, impatient with terminal programs and vocationalism, and a potential troublemaker. Some teachers in the college, even without the doctoral degree, have been considered overtrained; that is, thought to be too centered on one academic specialty and shy on the flexibility and tolerance needed for performance in the instructional role. The common organizational requirement of being able to get along with the rest of the staff includes in this case some minimum rapport with vocational teachers, most of whom have had little or no college education. Of the dozen half-time teachers shared with Technical High in the fourth year, ten had no college degree; besides, the administrative staff itself, save one person, had not pursued formal education past the master's degree. Formal education to the point of a doctoral degree is thus not only regarded as unnecessary for teachers but as divisive, given the composition of the total staff and the location of the college in a public school system. It is therefore thought advisable not to have too many Ph.D.'s on the staff.

With this, it is not to be expected that the typical staff member will be oriented to scholarship. The values of the system are against it. Even more than in those four-year colleges that prefer not to have their instructors engaged in research, the junior college expects work to be oriented to students. Research and writing are not encouraged and the load of other activities leaves little time. A questionnaire item asked whether the instructor had had professional writings published. Answers showed that sixty-two out of ninety staff members, or 69 per cent, had done no professional writing at any time in their career. However, six members of the staff had written books or monographs, and twenty-four had published articles of some kind. Thus professional writing was not unknown but was pursued only by few.

The instructional orientation imposed by formal rules and by the criteria of selection is not capricious but relates to certain job requirements, as seen by administrators and as worked out in practice. Sharply put, the basic requirement of the instructor is his ability to understand and manage the unselected aggregation of students in the typical classroom. Given the student characteristics reviewed in Chapter 2, it is clear that most teachers of the college must work with a large number of poorly equipped students as well as with highly qualified ones. For this central task, obscured by the "college" label, the teacher needs a will and a way, a conviction that the less qualified students properly belong in a "college" classroom, and an ability to manage students of widely varying aptitudes and interest. Both the conviction and the ability can be found in the ranks of public school teachers, but only infrequently, it can safely be said, in the academic communities of higher education.[15]

A point can be made here about the dilemma of the teacher in the junior college classroom. When a college does not screen students at the time of entry, classroom performance itself becomes the major means of screening. The sorting and winnowing-out process is thrown more into the classroom in junior colleges than in selective colleges. One problem of the instructor then is to help actively in identifying the true transfers and the latent terminal students and in pressuring the latter to recognize their status. Operationally, this means the teacher is asked to fail or give low grades to a much larger percentage of students than that sanctioned by the grading curve widely used elsewhere. Harsh grading is called for to give students, in a student body of lower than average aptitude, a correct appraisal of their ability in terms of transfer possibilities. As indicated in Chapter 2,

[15] The ideal junior college teacher, as reported in the junior college literature, is free of many characteristics of the academic person. In one study, poor junior college teachers were characterized by administrators in seventy-two different colleges as "warped scholars instead of teachers," "coming from the graduate schools and tending to be crushed under the weight of pedantry," "subject-matter conscious," and similarly. See David B. Pugh and Roy E. Morgan, "Faculty Needs and Requirements," *Junior College Journal*, vol. 13, pp. 427–435, May, 1943.

unless this is done, students will obtain the grades that allow them to transfer elsewhere, there to encounter a downgrading. Thus the instructor faces classrooms where wholesale failing is indicated, if the junior college is to allow only those of requisite ability to pass. Even for a teacher oriented to do so, this is a difficult stance to maintain. It establishes tension with the students and excites counterpressures from them. Teachers in San Jose Junior College indicate that failing is done with trepidation, and is not an openly encouraged policy of the administration. Besides, such a mandate is not readily accepted by the teacher who is committed to the viewpoint, common in the public schools, that each student should be treated on the basis of his own combination of abilities and helped to progress in some way. The conflict between standards and sympathy for the student is apparently much more acute than in other colleges.

It is most difficult for administrators to get across the nature of the student body and the nature of the teaching operation to new and prospective teachers, unless the teacher is from the public schools where he would have had experience with comprehensive student bodies. Without this background, a grasp and appreciation of the task of the junior college must be learned, against the expectations normally brought to college teaching. Most students are not college students in the sense familiar to four-year colleges and universities, and the properly oriented instructor is one who, at a minimum, (1) accepts the fact that the college has unselected students and (2) accepts the terminal operation as a legitimate, worthwhile enterprise.[16]

We now turn to some questionnaire results that indicate what the teachers think about their junior college positions. It was said earlier that high-school-trained teachers are predominantly

[16] For a description of criteria of personnel selection in another junior college, reflecting a "local community" philosophy, see Elbert K. Fretwell, Jr., *Founding Public Junior Colleges*, Bureau of Publications, Teachers College, Columbia University, New York, 1954, pp. 80–81.

recruited because they are expected to see the junior college student in a more favorable light than college teachers normally would. Interesting in this regard are the responses to an open-end question: "All things considered, what do you personally like *best* about teaching (working) in a junior college?" The most frequent response cited favorable characteristics of junior college students as compared with high school students. More than a third of the respondents remarked spontaneously on this, generally to the point that the students were more mature:

> Age level of students. Absence of pressure to "pass" students who do not meet standards of the courses.
>
> The students, on the whole, are more mature; they *want* to pursue knowledge.
>
> Students in voluntary attendance.
>
> Maturity of students. Opportunity to teach advanced courses in field.
>
> Relative academic freedom, and the opportunity to work with such adult students as might appear.
>
> Working with older students. Can delve more into subject area of interest.
>
> The opportunity to help hitherto undirected students.
>
> More mature student attitudes.
>
> Students more interested. Not compelled to attend.
>
> Compared to high school the junior college is more businesslike.
>
> The absence of a discipline problem (as compared with teaching in high school).

The point is clear that a high school frame of reference makes certain characteristics of junior college students appealing to their teachers. The responses of the few teachers with a background of college teaching, to the question of what they liked best, were generally of a different order:

> Close teacher-pupil relationship seldom possible at undergraduate level in larger colleges.
>
> Personal contact with students is on a different basis from either high-school or four-year-college contact.
>
> Broad curricula.
>
> One can feel much closer and important to the student than in the stiffer, colder climate of a four-year college.

Here it was personal relations in a smaller college that seemed most important. Apparently there was also more strain in simply saying something favorable: one answer was "it's a job," and two of the three teachers not responding at all to this question had a college background.

Similarly, the answers to more highly structured attitude questions would indicate that the college-background personnel were less sympathetic to the nature of the junior college student body than were those trained by the public schools. Table 20 reports twelve questions, out of forty analyzed, on which persons with these two types of background were most divergent in point of view (there was more than a 20 per cent difference in the amount of agreement with the question). The more supportive view of those with public school background is seen in a number of questions; questions 4, 5, 9, 10, and 11 all bear closely on junior college students. In question 4, those with a public school background are willing to see the junior college related to "non-academically inclined" undergraduates, but those of college background reject this definition. Only the college-trained members of the staff, to the extent of 50 per cent or more, believe that entrance requirements are too low (question 5), that there is too much stress on quantity of students and not enough on quality (question 9), and that junior college students are not mature and interested (question 10). The differences are consistently in the direction of the teachers with public school experience having attitudes that support the college's unselected

Table 20

Differences in the Point of View of Junior College Personnel, by Public School and College Background, San Jose Junior College (In per cent)

Question response	Previous experience: Public school (N = 66)		Previous experience: College (N = 10)*	Previous experience: None (N = 14)	Total (N = 90)
Agree that:					
(1) junior college instruction is usually as good as, if not better than, the *lower-division* teaching in most four-year colleges and universities.	86	(56)†	30	79	79
(2) the junior college is usually closer to the needs of the community than is the four-year college or university.	83	(53)	30	93	79
(3) the junior college is too oriented to "life adjustment" education.	12	(38)	50	14	17
(4) an important function of the junior college should be to relieve the four-year college and university of their considerable burden of nonacademically inclined undergraduates.	63	(34)	29	40	55
(5) scholastic entrance requirements for junior colleges are too low for the most part.	39	(31)	70	36	42
(6) four-year colleges and universities play too great a role in determining junior college programs.	30	(30)	0	21	26

Table 20 (*Continued*)

Question response	Previous experience				Total (N = 90)
	Public school (N = 66)		College (N = 10)*	None (N = 14)	
(7) the administration of a junior college is more likely to give recognition to a good teacher than is a four-year college or university.	39	(29)	10	50	39
(8) the junior college is too much like a glorified high school.	21	(29)	50	7	22
(9) there is too much stress in the junior college on quantity of students and not enough on quality of students.	32	(28)	60	14	32
(10) junior college students generally are more mature and interested in pursuing their education.	63	(23)	40	64	61
(11) students are frequently "overcounseled" in a junior college.	11	(22)	33	0	11
(12) prefer to teach in junior college rather than four-year college or university.	44	(22)	22	39	41

* The number of responses was nine instead of ten for questions 4, 11, and 12.

† Difference between those with public school background and those with four-year-college or university experience.

SOURCE: Junior college teacher questionnaire.

type of student body. The teachers with no previous experience, it may be noted, generally answered in the same way as did those with public school experience. Having taught in a four-year college or university appears here as the source of greatest disaffection about the student. Besides, the staff members with this background had been selected for employment in the college and had remained with it. They would probably have adapted to the nature of the college in considerable degree and hence not be as unsupportive in outlook as an outside four-year-college or university teacher.

The staff of the college, however, was by no means enchanted with their students. In response to the open-end question of what the staff member liked least about working in a junior college, the second most frequent answer was a criticism of the student. (Most frequent was criticism of work conditions, discussed below.) More than twenty answers (out of ninety) were as follows: "too many noncollege-caliber students"; "necessity of 'spoon-feeding' students who are actually incapable of college work"; "transient nature of students"; "many are lazy"; "the diversity of abilities, backgrounds, and motivation in the student body"; "unrealistic objectives of most students." None of these quoted answers were from teachers with college backgrounds. A similar type of response was spontaneously elicited by another open-end question as to the "most important single problem junior colleges face today." The most frequent answer (21 per cent) cited the "inferior caliber" of students or the range of student abilities:

> The academic programs may be watered down to accommodate the inferior students who must legally be admitted.
>
> Lack of standards. Anyone can enter, fail, and continue to do so indefinitely, which is demoralizing to school, instructors, and the better students.
>
> How adequately to educate students whose ability range is so broad.
>
> Student attitude toward class work.
>
> Too many students with unrealistic goals.
>
> Having the terminal and the transfer students in the same classes.

> Adapting programs to wide range of students who come.
>
> Educational retardation of large proportion of the student body, e.g., low reading achievement.

Again, none of these responses were from the college-background teachers. There was, then, a heavy volume of criticism about students from even those that had the "best-fitting" background.

In a number of cases, characteristics of the students were both the most liked and the least liked features of the college in the eyes of teachers. A teacher who found that "generally speaking the students are interested in learning" also held that "too many [are] noncollege-caliber students"; a teacher who enjoyed "working with people who have ability but poor previous records" was unhappy about their "transient nature"; and one who liked most the fact that "at junior college you work more closely with the students," liked least that there are "too many students to lead around by the hand." Clearly in such a diverse student body there is a lot from which to choose. There is also a high degree of interest in the nature of the student body, pro and con, as evidenced by "students" being a frequent response to both the "like best" and the "like least" questions.

Turning from characteristics of the students to characteristics of the task of teaching, as analytically distinct features of the college, again we seem to find the junior college standing well for those with a high school frame of reference. In responding to what they "like best about teaching (working) in a junior college," many teachers spontaneously referred to greater freedom and more advanced teaching:

> Opportunity to teach more advanced material in my subject field.
>
> Flexibility of specific course content.
>
> Relative academic freedom, and the opportunity to work with such adult students as might appear.

> Freedom of one's schedule; enjoyment of teaching the specific subject area most desired.
>
> Freedom in the classroom re subject matter.
>
> The opportunity to expound in an adult way in any subject field. Impossible to do this in high school.

Already used to a comprehensive student body, the high-school-background teachers seemed to see the college as a place where they have (1) greater freedom in teaching and (2) older students. They were now offering "college-level instruction, individualized," and with this they were more willing than those of college background to agree that the instructional work was of a high order. The question in Table 20 showing greatest disagreement between staff members with these two types of background (question 1) was one that compared junior college instruction with that of the first two years of four-year colleges and universities. The "public-school teachers" overwhelmingly (86 per cent) agreed that junior college instruction was as good if not better, but only three out of ten "college teachers" would assent to this. Questions 7 and 8 also suggest a more positive perception by those trained in public schools (see Table 20). Question 12 is of special interest: "If you had your choice, and if salary schedules, promotion opportunities, retirement benefits, job security, etc., were equal in each type of educational institution, in which would you prefer to teach (work)?" Junior college, four-year college, university, and high school were provided as alternatives. Preferring to teach in junior college were 44 per cent of the staff with public school experience, 22 per cent of those with college background, 39 per cent of those with no experience, and 41 per cent of the total staff. Thus of these categories, the "public school members" preferred the junior college the most and the "college members" preferred it the least. The most enlightening of these figures is the one for the total staff, which indicates that six out of ten staff members would prefer to teach in a senior college. In comparison with the fifty-two who had this preference, one respondent chose the high school. The identification "upward" appeared strong, the four-year college and university appearing attractive to the college's staff for status reasons, if for no other.

But, as with student characteristics, the more positive orientation toward the college of those with public school experience did not mean they were in accord with existing requirements and practices. In criticizing the college, conditions of teaching were most frequently referred to, even more so than student characteristics. The feature least liked about the college was the work load:

> Teaching load far too heavy (24 hours per week in Business).
>
> Overload in four different fields, with not enough time to do any one job efficiently.
>
> Large work load does not permit proper course development.
>
> Wasted time in unnecessary clerical work. Teaching load 18 hours for lecture courses, with as high as 5 preparations.
>
> Having to teach so many subjects at one time.

All these were responses of "public school teachers"; altogether about thirty responses of this kind were made. The responses suggest that when high school teachers become junior college teachers they define themselves as college teachers and take the senior college rather than the high school as the standard for evaluating work requirements. They stand ready in at least some aspects to shed the public school way of life, but in general the administrative setting of their new positions prevents them from doing so.

We may close this excursion into teacher attitudes by reviewing the reactions of the college's staff to two questions that were not reported in either Table 16 or Table 20. To a general question on the way the person "feels" about working in the college, 72 per cent of the total staff responded that they were well or completely satisfied. Subdivided by type of experience, satisfied were: of those with college background, 60 per cent; of those of public school experience, 73 per cent; and of the no-experience personnel, 79 per cent. By type of college position: 63 per cent of applied teachers, 75 per cent of academic teachers, and 80 per cent of administrators. As was consistently true for many questions, the two groups furthest apart were the college-background staff members, nearly all of whom were academic teachers, and the administrators, none of whom had a college background. The satisfaction level of the staff overall was close to that of junior college personnel generally. The same question in a national survey showed 79 per cent satisfied,[17] which is not much different from the 72 per cent for the college. But in neither case does it appear that this "satisfaction" question is an index of a deep-seated satisfaction. As was reported earlier, 59 per cent of the college's staff indicated a preference to teach in a four-year college or university; on the same question in the national survey, 52 per cent of more than 3,200 respondents said that they preferred the higher colleges.[18] Apparently the San Jose teachers are similar to those elsewhere—they are "satisfied, but. . . ."

One other question contributes to our interpretation here, being especially illuminating on the value placed on the junior college by its own staff. A question was posed nationally and in San Jose as follows:

> Assume that you have a son who wants, and is competent, to complete four years of college education. Assume further that finances are no problem. Now all things considered, which of the following alternatives do you lean to:

[17] Medsker, *op. cit.*, chap. 7.

[18] *Ibid.*

He attend a four-year college or university for four years.
He attend a junior college for two years and then transfer to a four-year college or university.

a) Why?

Nationally, 41 per cent said they would send their son to the junior college first.[19] In San Jose this response fell off sharply to 26 per cent. Again, the extremes within the junior college were college-background teachers (20 per cent) and the administrators (40 per cent), and as indicated by the latter figure, no subcategory had a majority with this preference. This would seem to indicate that many junior college teachers, especially in San Jose, do not rate the junior college as high as the senior colleges for the good student. When cost is ruled out, they recommend the four-year centers. This would seem to leave the junior college, in the teacher's image, as a place for those that lack the money or the aptitude or both.

[19] Medsker, *op. cit.*, chap. 7.

CHAPTER 4
The Mass College

The tendencies that had crystallized in San Jose Junior College by the end of its first four years cannot be said to have fixed the nature of the college for all time, for some evolution would later occur and radical transformations are always possible. Yet we have seen certain orientations and practices to be so much a part of the organization that they could be expected to shape its future development. The determinants of the college's emerging character, moreover, were fixed in its context, beyond self-determination, so that barring a radical shift in setting, the early trends were firmly anchored. The preceding chapters have attempted to identify these organizational tendencies and the conditions that promoted them. This chapter offers a fuller interpretation of organization character, directly of this one college and indirectly of other colleges that operate under similar conditions.

ORGANIZATION CHARACTER[1]

Organization character is a complex matter, often hidden from public view. It may be identified in part by obtaining answers

[1] For a general discussion of the concept of organization character, see Philip Selznick, *Leadership in Administration*, Row, Peterson & Company, Evanston, Ill., 1957, pp. 38–55.

to the following questions: Is the organization independent of or dependent upon its environment; and if the latter, on whom is it dependent? What is the general orientation of the organization's programs and relationships? Does the organization have a distinctive way of life? What can the organization do? What degree of competence can be expected in the performance of tasks? What general roles does it assume within a larger scheme?

Administrative Dependency

No organization is free of environmental influence, but a highly independent firm, agency, or school can be inner-directed for the most part. The placement of San Jose Junior College within a unified district of the California public schools renders it an administratively dependent organization. In key policy matters its administrators are subordinate to the central authorities of the district. Financial control, personnel selection, and other basic operational matters of a junior college in a unified or high school district may be handled by the district or delegated to the college at the district's discretion. In San Jose the district chose to exercise considerable control, and in respect to many means of developing an organizational orientation, the college was clearly not its own boss. Then, in addition to dependency on the local district, the administrative placement of the college also rendered it dependent on certain fundamental provisions of the state public school system. Central here was the *state* definition of junior college clientele, because this determined that the college would have little discretion in building its social base. The choice of selecting certain kinds of students for admission, for example, was not open to the college. The experience reported in Chapters 1 to 3 amply demonstrates the high degree of administrative dependency.

The relationship of the college to the local district, and at a second remove to the state public school system, is permanent in its general form. The specific degree of dependency is more problematic and subject to change. Compared with the time of its origin, the college gained some strength a few years later in certain areas of authority. Its ever-growing enrollment meant that as an administrative unit the college was the largest component of the district, approaching in size the combined enrollment of all San Jose high schools. With this, its voice in district affairs could hardly remain subdued. Its sizable staff began to make itself heard, and the directorship of the college became a position of some importance. Eventually, the college could also hope to gain some support from local business as it became more widely known as a source of trained personnel. Besides, in a rapidly growing metropolitan area, there is always some interest in more college facilities.

But all these changes did not remove the college from the unified district. Within this structure, the controlling board must continue to consider the interests of the other departments of the system and bring the college into a system-wide equilibrium. Barring a virtual breakdown in district administration, members of the superintendent's staff remain the ultimate arbitrators among the professional personnel. Their control of personnel assignment and budget allocation insures that the district will be unified in operation as well as in name. Thus the dependent relationship of the college to local public school officials remains intrinsic to its administrative location. It would be changed only by a drastic move that would pull the college out of the district and place it in a different type of control structure. Only one alternative is provided in California—a separate local district for the junior college alone. This form of school government clearly reduces administrative dependency and hence is generally desired by junior college personnel. But such a change is not likely in San Jose and in the metropolitan areas of the state generally. Where the tax base (assessed valuation) of existing city districts readily supports a junior college, the integration of junior college management with that of the elementary schools and high schools is highly probable.

Dependency on Unselected Base

Administrative dependency is common for subordinate units within an organization. While frequently overlooked in the consideration of educational problems and its meaning not always understood, it can be readily identified. The control of a headquarters over a field office is relatively easy to see, partly because the relationship is highly structured. Not so apparent, however, is the influence on an organization from an unorganized source. The relationship is diffuse and likely to escape participants as well as outsiders. A second dependency pattern of San Jose Junior College is of this kind and is of primary importance in its character. In Chapter 2 it was pointed out that the principal features of the college's student body were beyond its control. Membership in the student body is completely open to the general public. Once within the doors, students choose courses and majors within wide ranges, although the college attempts to exercise some control through counseling and guidance. But overall the college is directly shaped by virtually unlimited student choice of admission and participation. As a result, the size and composition of the student body and the shape of the college's programs are not in an important sense controlled or consciously determined by anyone. Effects of the self-selecting student body were seen in Chapter 3 to go past the curriculum to shape the formal structure and the instructional staff. Few features of the organization escape some determination by attributes of the student body as a whole.

Decisive in establishing dependency on this kind of student base was the organization's lack of discretion in being able to decide whom it would serve and what kind of education it would offer. This authority rested with the state and the district, and through their definition of the open door, the student body was made an active force. Direction by students occurs most completely when a junior college is new. Once a character is formed it has a momentum of its own, and later generations of students do not find the organization so open to influence by student choice. Orientations of a college, such as its emphasis on certain programs, become built-in and somewhat resistant to change. But the exposure of a college to a nonselected pool of students will always entail a relatively high degree of adaptability, compared with colleges based on selected, constructed constituencies, because the college is placed in a reacting rather than initiating position.

Secondary School Orientation

Related to the college's twofold dependency on district and students was its emerging secondary-school perspective. To tend in outlook more toward the high school than to four-year colleges and universities is natural in the college's setting, because its administration places it in a public school "society" and at the same time removes it from the direct impact of other kinds of colleges. It has been seen that the college is controlled and operated by a local board and financed by local and state funds in ways virtually identical to that of the public high school. Its administrative and instructional staffs were largely trained in secondary education and are expected to follow public school procedures. It is open to everyone and serves as a comprehensive school, incorporating, in a sense, "noncollege" students as well as those normally defined as college students. As a result, its student body has the heterogeneity of ability and interest found in the public high school. Besides, the college is geared to local conditions. For the San Jose area it is assuming tasks that were previously and still are partly performed by the public high school: providing terminal occupational training at home, preparing and filtering candidates for study in four-year colleges, and counseling on occupational choice and academic promise. Its terminal work includes curricula shifted to it from the local high schools. In operation as well as in formal existence, it is the "capstone," a term used by junior college advocates, of the local public school system.

The contrast with the university and four-year college concerning these features is striking. As mentioned in the introduction, the "higher" public colleges are controlled by state-wide boards and financed by state funds. The public junior college is the only unit of public higher education appearing in large number which is locally governed. The instructional staffs of the senior colleges are recruited from their own realm, and training in the public schools is more likely to be held against a senior college teacher than considered a virtue. Similarly, administrative training and experience are of a different order in the two types of colleges, with preparation in a school of education differently valued. In respect to admissions, four-year colleges and universities are generally selective and hence not open to everyone. They do not embrace the notion of being comprehensive schools for all. Besides, they do not normally commit themselves to vocational programs of less than four-year's duration as alternatives to the traditional definition of attending college. Then, too, their student bodies are generally recruited from the state and the nation rather than from the local neighborhood alone.

Such differences between a junior college and the other better-known forms of college organization are bound to create a basic difference in total orientation. The magnitude of this difference was suggested in the discussion of the ideal teacher in Chapter 3. In common with many other junior colleges, the San Jose Junior College avoids the university man, the instructor oriented toward research and scholarship and considered impatient with the poor student. On this score, the college finds the four-year-college teacher also too much influenced by the traditional image of college as a place for selected students. Along with other public junior colleges, the San Jose Junior College does not pretend to approximate a "community of scholars." It aspires to have personnel oriented to teaching, counseling, and local affairs, and personnel sympathetic to student bodies in the thirteenth and fourteenth grades of the public schools. It more closely reflects a public school emphasis on the instructor as teacher-counselor. How far removed it is from the image of the educational enterprise acclaimed in universities, and somewhat in colleges, may be suggested by two statements of ideals by university administrators. The first is a definition of the university by James B. Conant: "A university is a community of scholars, with a considerable degree of independence and self-government, concerned with professional education, the advancement of knowledge, and the general education of the leading citizens." [2] "Community of scholars," "considerable degree of independence," "advancement of knowledge," "general education of the leading citizens"—such conceptions are indeed alien to the place and nature of the junior college. Junior colleges do not talk this language, nor do the public schools generally, of course.

A second statement is by Theodore C. Blegen, from his analysis of problems of the State University of New York: "A teaching institution that affords no place to research and gives research no encouragement and support defeats itself. It defeats itself because in effect it denies the need for self-education by its own faculty." [3] Such a statement helps to highlight similarities and differences in definitions of the work of the teacher. The importance of research is generally accepted in the state university, debated in four-year colleges, and little if ever considered in the junior college and the public schools. The self-image of the San

[2] James B. Conant, *Education in a Divided World,* Harvard University Press, Cambridge, Mass., 1948, p. 158.

[3] Theodore C. Blegen, *The Harvests of Knowledge: A Report on Research Potentials and Problems in the State University of New York,* The Research Foundation of State University of New York, Albany, N.Y., 1957, p. 8.

Jose Junior College is far from such ideals. In the college, the tasks and symbols of scholarship and research have only peripheral relevance to what is expected of the organization.

Nevertheless, the San Jose Junior College has some orientations not characteristic of public schools and some university-type procedures. Teachers are freer than in high school, because they may fail students rather than having to put up with them. There is a tendency for teachers to identify "upward" toward the four-year college and university, claiming parallel work, rather than "downward" toward the high school. This amounts at times to an attempt to think of the school as a college-preparatory academy. Some staff members are interested in high academic standards and scholarly publication. But these tendencies can wax only within the limits of the situation, as set by the clientele, the rules for relating to them, the public school system, and the fact that the college administration must largely operate as an arm of district management. Notable is the limitation on scholarly study and research set by the time investment in teaching and counseling. The work with students tends to be a total work performance for the teacher.

Diffuse Commitment

Organization character may vary greatly in degree of distinctiveness, which is generally gained by selective commitment and special symbols. A private college may combine a particular history of denominational support with a special constituency, take pride in specific campus buildings and noted graduates, and claim a type of undergraduate life not possessed by any other college. Above all, distinctive character is based on selective work and special competence.

The emerging character of San Jose Junior College is relatively indistinct. Like most other public schools, its commitments are diffuse rather than selective. The college depends financially on the local tax-paying public and serves a broad-base clientele.

Hence its social bases are diffuse compared to colleges that lean on more narrowly defined supports. As a public school, the college is expected to provide many kinds of services for many kinds of people, particularly tailoring its curricula to the needs of diverse students. It rapidly became part of its character to think in broad comprehensive terms about multiple functions. Some of its operations, such as terminal vocational education and part-time adult education, are undefined in limit, expandable according to demand, and hence especially subject to diffusion. The character of the college has been moving toward that of a community college.

The character of the college is also relatively "unspecial" in the sense of sharing many attributes with other junior colleges of the state system and with locally controlled junior colleges in many parts of the country. It is one of a kind among sixty-odd colleges in the state, for example, and, like a public high school, it can hardly maintain that it is very different from the other members of its tribe, especially when it aspires to provide the array of services typical of the others. It is different in its area of location and somewhat different in being near to a state college, but not on other grounds. In public education the bases for distinctiveness are not readily available to most organizations. They are expected to be reasonably standardized units.

By its diffuse nature, San Jose Junior College is somewhat freer to adjust purposes and programs within wide limits than it would be if it were a specialized school. It is not selectively tied to an academic program alone, or to a completely vocational one, or to a particular class of students. It is free to move within an open range of activities as a changing environment indicates. More readily than the narrowly committed school, it can be in succession primarily a vocational school, an adult center, and a preparatory college. Each function is already a part of its comprehensive activity, and no unalterable selective commitments exist to bar a shift in emphasis. Nationally, the public junior college has demonstrated this flexibility; "special and adult students" reached 60 per cent of the total enrollment in the nation's junior colleges in 1944, at a time of shortage of regular students.[4] This aspect of flexibility in the character of comprehensive schools, not always apparent from the outside, is one to which school administrators are generally sensitive. This flexibility in the public schools is perhaps somewhat analogous to the policy of diversification in plant and product practiced by American business firms to enhance security in a changing environment.

The character of San Jose Junior College may be summarized in these terms: It is a relatively dependent organization, coming under direct control of a superior educational authority and compelled to react to a clientele not of its making. Its unselected student body determines the nature of its work and the evolution of its programs. It is oriented by context toward the outlook and operating modes of American secondary education and has taken on the multiplicity of commitments expected of a comprehensive school. Its tasks are diffuse and flexibly organized, producing an indistinct character when compared to schools that specialize in clientele and curricula. Its ability to react to an unselected social base is particularly noteworthy.

The characteristics of dependency on unselected base and diffusion in commitment may be widely observed in other public junior colleges, especially in the California system. Administrative subordination varies elsewhere according to the control structures in which junior colleges are located. The integrated forms of district control, where the junior college is administered together with other public schools, are most likely to parallel the San Jose findings. Separately administered junior college districts are at a first remove from this degree of administrative dependency, subordinating the junior college only to its own

[4] Jesse P. Bogue, *The Community College*, McGraw-Hill Book Company, Inc., New York, 1950, p. 35.

lay board. The characteristic of secondary school orientation, in turn, should be strongest in the integrated colleges and somewhat less strong, typically, in the more independent colleges. But in all control systems that represent local authority there is likely to be a strong tendency toward a secondary school orientation. In contrast, junior colleges directly administered by state educational systems will probably be relatively autonomous from local influences, with less secondary school orientation. Furthest removed from public school influence, of course, is the junior college administered as part of a university or state college, where formal dependency will tend to result in a traditional college orientation. It is the forms of local control that predispose toward a common-school model.

Clearly the problem of where to locate junior colleges administratively is more than a question of efficient, economical ordering of educational effort, of a logical structuring of school government. Since administrative place shapes the character of schools, it affects educational values. A particular type of location, such as the local school district, will accentuate certain programs and play down others, instill one outlook while obstructing another. The logical place for junior colleges, therefore, depends on the values that one wishes to implement.

The characteristics mentioned above as least likely to vary among public junior colleges were (1) unselected base and (2) diffuse commitment. These are also the organizational features which suggest classification of the public junior college under a general organizational type, the mass enterprise. There are schools other than the junior college, and organizations in other fields, that are also diffusely related to unselected, relatively undifferentiated clienteles.

A Special Ability

The character of an organization enables it to engage in certain tasks and disqualifies it from engaging in others. The San

Jose Junior College tends toward the need of ability to manage a heterodox, self-selecting student body. It is in the business of exposing a large student body of below-average college aptitude to some education beyond the high school. This exposure prepares a minority of the students to transfer after one or two years to a four-year college or university, principally the nearby state college. Some of these students are persons of ability who had poor academic records in high schools and were thus "salvaged" [5] for higher education by the junior college. But since most students terminate, and do so largely against their original hopes, the college particularly needs skill in disabusing students of their notions of transferring and in inducing them to accept a two-year alternative.

One competence which a junior college develops, therefore, is a general ability to react to an heterogenous free-forming clientele with diverse programs. The ability to handle diversity, however, militates against a high degree of competence in any one educational effort, such as the vocational or the college-preparatory alone. San Jose Junior College cannot be a highly intellectualized academy or a first-rate technical school, because its trade school commitment will not allow it to be an academy and its college-preparation work will not permit a full flowering of a technical orientation. In short, ability lies not in a distinctive educational specialty; competence lies in balancing disparate operations and in providing the means of student movement from one operation to another.

This brings us to the college's operational specialty, its most important feature: the specific operation of transforming transfer students into terminal students. Since the movement of students in the college must be principally away from the transfer

[5] Junior college advocates refer to a "salvage function" in enumerating advantages of the public junior college. Salvaging lost talent is a claim that links the work of the junior college to several national concerns, e.g., the full utilization of manpower and equality of opportunity.

work, the efficacy of the college is especially defined by its ability to reassign the student from a transfer to a terminal major without losing him in the process. Junior colleges in general have found this difficult. Four-year colleges and universities do not have this task, because they do not include short-term terminal alternatives. High schools do not overlap the college years, hence do not have the problem either.

When the question is asked, what can a junior college do that other schools cannot do, one answer is that it can manage the latent terminal student who wants to embark on a college education, but who would not, at the most, get past the first two years. For this type of student, the junior college provides short-term vocational and general educational programs as alternatives to the usual curricula, as well as two years of college work per se. Besides, the junior college provides an inexpensive two years of college-credit work for the few students who will proceed to other schools and short-term programs for the students who always had terminal intentions.

THE SOCIAL BASE OF THE MASS COLLEGE

The intriguing feature of San Jose Junior College and the public junior college generally is the relationship to an outside base of operations composed of a large, undifferentiated aggregation of potential students or clients. This characteristic, central to what will be called the mass enterprise, meaningfully differentiates organizations in education from one another, and also serves as a way of understanding some organizational similarities between such common distinctions as political, economic, and educational organization. The student constituency of San Jose Junior College showed itself as an active force in determining the practices of the college; it showed itself as such to a degree not normally anticipated when one considers who determines policies in American schools and colleges. This active nature of a student body seems to be related to the college's dependency on an amorphous social base. How? We are used to organized pressure, to intervention, and to direction by professional staff, but how does an unorganized influence operate? What happens when the students, collectively and without intention, heavily condition the college?

A matter of first importance for the influence of the student body on the policies of any educational institution is the extent and kind of selection of students exercised by the institution. Selectivity makes possible a structuring of clientele. Selection is a control device, allowing participation only within certain limits. Such control is evident in private colleges, which selectively cultivate a social base and structure their clientele. They establish ties with certain families, social groups, and feeder schools. Selectivity in such cases reduces the need of the institution to adjust to undifferentiated constituencies, and gives to participation a certain distinction. In general, then, the form and content of an aggregation of students entering a college is determined largely by the extent to which the college itself can select. Is the student body to be of low, medium, or high social status? Strongly or weakly motivated? Of high or low aptitude? The selective school can tailor a constituency that supports the self-imposed ideals of the school authorities. Even a college that is temporarily unselective can affect the nature of its student body if it has a strong self-image to bring to bear.

But the educational organization that is permanently unselective has little choice in defining a student body and depends on the fortunes of its environment. With nonselection comes a weakening of control and an enlarging of the discretion of potential students. Participation is "open." The form and content of an entering student body are then free-forming, as far as organizational control is concerned. Nonselection is the most essential condition under which students impose their collective will on a junior college.

Secondly, the extent to which participation is voluntary affects the influence of the student body on the character of a college. Older students are more often voluntary than younger ones. When students pass the age of compulsory school attendance, usually at sixteen, the relation between students and the school changes. Past this age and especially past high school graduation, the student is set free, granted greater choice in attending, and made less subject to the control of school personnel. He can give, change, or withhold his participation. If he also has the right to enter a nonselective college, then his voluntariness becomes an active force. He can decide for himself whether and when he will enter and actively contend for his own version of the ends and means of his education. The conjunction of nonselection and age above compulsory schooling in the public junior college gives maximum thrust to the choices and characteristics of students.

One consequence of these conditions is the college's vulnerability to the competition of attractive alternatives. In the lower grades, students are usually not free to shift from one school to another; student bodies are nearly always fixed by the jurisdiction of school districts. But after high school, competition enters. The voluntary students are mobile, allowed to choose among schools and programs. The nonselective college faces specialized, selective competitors, drawing off good students from the local population and from the college's own student body. The other colleges are generally free to manipulate their own admission standards in the light of their own interests; they may attempt to take only the most promising students if there are many such students available, or they may go to the bottom of the barrel when the supply of students is low. The nonselective school must passively take what comes to it. The junior college competes in other ways, however, by inexpensiveness, convenience of location, and an adaptive array of programs. Programs can be manipulated from year to year, and the pressure of competition on the mass college is to be adaptable and attractive to the diversity of students who make their appearance. The result, again, is to enhance student impact on the college.

A third major consideration in the influence of the student clientele is the nature of the processing of people in a junior college. Like other schools and like such institutions as the social agency, hospital, and prison, the junior college works on people rather than on objects. Students *flow through* the organization; they are not sold a product or given a service, as in a business firm and in most public and private service organizations. The students are acted upon in the work of the school, and the students, in turn, shape the tasks of work; they are organizational participants, intervening from within. We should expect such a people-work organization to be extensively affected by attributes of its clientele, including their intentions. But decisive for the character of the organization is the extent to which the client participants are controlled. How to control a clientele that is always within the doors is a general problem faced by all organizations that work on people. One answer is the asserting of professional authority and the defining of the client participant as incompetent to decide what treatment he should receive. The hospital patient is defined as sick, the prison inmate is labeled as criminal; both are defined as having something wrong with them, hence are placed in special roles and withdrawn from normal activities. Their choices are narrowed and the authority of an organizational staff is extended over them. The extent of control varies greatly but there is no doubt about who knows best.

In schools, the participation of the student is a normal social role; there is no deviant status attached to the student as a basis for the school staff to assert control. Control over students is strong in many societies, however, as it was earlier in American education, on the ground that the educator, adult and experienced, knows better than the student what is proper for the student to learn and to do. Where the student is defined as immature and the teacher is seen to have the responsibility of instilling cultural principles and bodies of knowledge, then the desires and attributes of students are not likely to affect the character of schools. But tendencies of modern society change these assumptions. Even in the elementary school, the teacher becomes a more responsive agent, turning toward the needs and verbalized desires of students of diverse background for cues as to what shall be taught.[6] By the time the student enters secondary education, major choices as to avenues and forms of participation in school are open to him. The further he goes, the more the comprehensive school assumes a servicing role. The public junior college is at the point in educational structure where professional dictation is likely to be minimal. The students are not only unselected and voluntary participants, but they are older than those in the high schools and possess more of the rights of adults. Their needs go off in all directions: preparation for a number of diverse colleges, job training for a varied array of occupations, sophistication in such personal concerns as the responsibilities of marriage. The spectrum of possible concerns is wide and the comprehensive school is oriented to do as much as possible for all students. The student is granted much choice; student processing needs then to be responsively and flexibly organized, without regard to academic tradition and staff conceptions of the ultimate purpose and shape of the organization. Processing in a junior college is student-oriented in more than a superficial sense of the term.

An important feature of the flow of students through a junior college is the shortness of their stay. The in-and-out flux is always on a large scale in the two-year school. The vast majority do not remain even two years, earlier transferring to other colleges, going off to jobs, or just dropping out. This means the junior college must take on some of the coloration of a short-stay institution. Somewhat like such military units as the basic

[6] For a discussion of changes in the role of the teacher, see David Riesman, *The Lonely Crowd*, Yale University Press, New Haven, Conn., 1950, chap. 2.

training post, the classification center, and the replacement depot, the junior college processes batches of people who are here today and gone tomorrow. Unlike the military establishment, however, the college does not have firm control. Besides, the handling of large numbers who have a short stay cannot help but promote some mass-processing tendencies, such as classroom counseling, in order to get the job done. The student is not around long enough to allow for the slow development of identification with the college or gradual assimilation into a set of values different from what he has known before. The task is to do something for large numbers relatively quickly, in the first place to get them on a track appropriate to their ability. Proper classification is uppermost in importance. Then the students can be given some training in whatever time remains before they move out, a week to two years later. Since the leaving is voluntary, the college has no control over it. The self-selection in and out makes the college a "service" version of the classification and distribution center, doing what it can for those who will come to it and in the time they will grant. The need is to build processing systems for the major types of entrants, the latent terminal student being the most difficult type.

This exploratory review of the relationship of the junior college to its students, actual and potential, leads to a general conclusion. As a consequence of dependency on an unselective-voluntary clientele, such a college will be extensively shaped by characteristics of the multitude. Of all types of schools, the unselective-voluntary type will be most open to wide clientele influence.[7] It has little opportunity to shape a social base and it has

[7] Using the two variables of selectivity and voluntariness of participation, three other major types are suggested: selective-voluntary membership (the private college, selective state universities); unselective-captive (the public elementary school and high school); selective-captive (the private elementary and secondary school). These broad categories offer a crude comparative framework and the examples are illustrative only. Only the type in which the public junior college falls is here discussed.

a strong organizational need to adapt to self-selective students.[8] The hands of its constituents are not tied by a compulsory status; the opposite might almost be said: the school is compelled by the kinds of students who elect to appear. The school can neither force students to attend, as in the early grades, nor choose a particular type of student as in the selective colleges. Being neither compulsory nor selective, the junior college faces a large educational market of free buyers, all or none of whom can choose to avail themselves of the opportunity.

In an earlier study, a similar kind of school was analyzed and termed "service enterprise."[9] This conception highlighted the adaptive response of the public adult school to changing clientele interests and the tendency of the adult education administrator to look to environment for direction rather than to self-determined purpose. Typical of American adult education is the transitory quality of participation of the part-time adult student and the immediacy of the organizational attempt to "service the demand." The concept of service enterprise connotes these features. The junior college, too, has attributes of a service enterprise, but it has a student body that is somewhat more involved and less changeable than that of the adult school. It has greater steadiness because it is part of an educational sequence for the young; hence, it does not need to be so immediately adaptable in insuring its survival. The notion of service is relevant but needs extension in order to point to other aspects of character and to be applicable to a wide class of organizations.

The concept of the mass enterprise, as developed in this study, appears to serve these requirements better. In the strictest sense, a mass enterprise is an organization whose character is defined

[8] On the need of the public schools generally to be increasingly adaptable as they undergo "democratization," see David Riesman, *Constraint and Variety in American Education*, University of Nebraska Press, Lincoln, Nebr., 1956, pp. 108–112.

[9] Burton R. Clark, *Adult Education in Transition: A Study of Institutional Insecurity*, University of California Press, Berkeley, Calif., 1956, chap. 4.

by dependency on a large, nonselected, voluntary clientele. In this sense, the term applies in its purest form to the junior college and the adult school. In both we find the faculty adapted to a mass character. The constraint of organization character in these schools begins with the unsolicited social bases on which they rest.

This definition of mass organization is different from the common use of "mass" to connote sheer numbers. It is also somewhat different from, although related to, the definition of mass organization in the sociological literature on "mass society." [10] In the latter, the mass organization is one in which a relatively unstructured membership participates weakly and without influence; with this goes a susceptibility of the membership to mobilization by leadership groups that know how to play upon emotional adherence. Such an organization is highly susceptible to totalitarian control. This sociological definition emphasizes an advanced or acute state of "massness," where the membership lends itself to manipulation and is ready to take on new ways of behaving. Typical here is the *activist* mass organization, one readily deployed by its leadership. The present study emphasizes a more *passive* form of mass organization, one controlled *by* the multitude rather than vice versa. Membership is relatively unstructured and participation is segmental, as in the activist organization, but mobilization by leadership is absent. Instead, leadership adapts to membership in a service fashion, induced to passivity by conditions that promote dependency.

In this sense many business firms and public bureaus are mass

[10] General discussion of mass society may be found in Karl Mannheim, *Man and Society in an Age of Reconstruction,* Harcourt, Brace and Company, Inc., New York, 1950, pp. 79–107; Emil Lederer, *State of the Masses,* W. W. Norton & Company, Inc., New York, 1940; C. Wright Mills, *The Power Elite,* Oxford University Press, New York, 1956, chap. 13; and Philip Selznick, *The Organizational Weapon,* McGraw-Hill Book Company, Inc., New York, 1952, chap. 7, which also offers a definition of mass organization, p. 286.

organizations, steered by the desires of a heterogeneous public. But generally such agencies do not purport to have a "nonmass" role and are not traditionally conceived to have broad social and cultural functions. Their adaptive responsiveness gives issue to no special social problems. But the attempt in modern democratic societies to adapt schools to the multitude is of a different order. Here core cultural values are at stake, because the schools have traditionally been defined as agents of the general society, transmitting a heritage and helping to bring the young to adulthood. The impact of mass organization on the role of the school needs extensive exploration. The mass enterprise in higher education contributes to a vast democratization, but it also entails a lowering of standards of admission and attainment. Its existence may be essential to the welfare of "nonmass" colleges, but at the same time it may change the nature of higher education by blurring its meaning and encouraging a sovereignty of the poorly qualified. Value judgments on the "worth" of the public junior college need to be made on complex grounds, weighing the pros and cons, for much more than money and administrative convenience are at issue.

CHAPTER 5

Roles and Problems of a Junior College

ORGANIZATION ROLES

Organization role is the performance of an organization that is associated with a place within a larger system. Roles are affected by the place assigned to an organization among other organizations and by the particular capacities that it develops through time. Roles may be designed or may emerge in unplanned ways. They may be manifest to participants and occasional observers or latent in the situation. Among the roles that come to view in this case study, some are fairly well known to educators, in part; but at least one major role, and sociologically the most interesting one, has not been previously identified, apparently because of its latency in the place and operation of the junior college.

One obvious and important role of the public junior college is the extending of education beyond the high school to academically less competent students. San Jose Junior College clearly performs in this way for the student population of its area, and unselective two-year colleges are likely to perform in this way wherever they exist. This broadening of participation in higher education entails a greater degree of openness in admission than is commonly recognized by the public and educators alike, with neither low ability nor low income preventing entry. The public junior college is a cutting edge of the democratization trend in American education because of its abolition of formal barriers. Part of the performance of San Jose Junior College in the San Jose area and of junior colleges generally is to enlarge the number of college openings in such a way as to make a college seat available on demand and without judgment on the student.

This role is supported by the outlook of state educational authorities in California, favoring some college education for all. This outlook was reflected in a study conducted by the Liaison Committee of the California State Board of Education and the Regents of the University of California in 1956, which showed that slightly more than one-half (56.4 per cent) of the June, 1955, graduates from public high schools in California did not meet the entrance requirements of the University of California or the state colleges. This was interpreted by the Joint Staff that prepared the study as a denial of equal educational opportunity:[1]

> The Joint Staff believes that the figures in the last two columns of this table [Number and Per Cent not Meeting Entrance Requirements of University or State Colleges] are of special significance, because they show that for 23,271 of the 41,423 June, 1955 high school graduates covered in the Table, the only opportunity of attending a publicly supported institution of higher education in the state is that provided by a junior college. Failure, then, to provide an adequate system of junior colleges throughout the state takes that opportunity away from some of these graduates. The Joint Staff is convinced that the provision of an adequate system of junior colleges is an essential part of the state's goal of guaranteeing

[1] *Study of Need*, p. 128.

> equal educational opportunity to all its citizens, as neither the state colleges nor the University should change objectives to render this service.

In this interpretation, public officials are morally obliged to provide a place in higher education for all applicants. To do less is seen as a denial of equal opportunity. Although this confuses equal opportunity with the extension of participation to all, it is in line with the popular reading of democratic ideals:[2] Persons seeking entry need not all be admitted to the same segment of higher education, but they must be admitted somewhere. The public junior college as the nonselective segment of the total college system, makes this "total" admission more than theoretically possible. In this performance, it caters to the mass of "unqualified" students.

In the role of opening wider the door to higher education in its area, San Jose Junior College also acts as a screening agent for other colleges. It handles a large number of local students, out of whom a few are filtered for the state university and a larger number for the nearby state college. It is part of a system of two-year units that now separates the bulk of lower-division students of the state from the four-year colleges. As is common throughout the state, most of these separated students are, in the filtering process, retained by the junior college, to be trained in one- and two-year programs if they will remain with the college. But trained or not, these students leave "college" without having touched the four-year centers.

In this performance, the junior college becomes the proper

[2] For a similar interpretation by educators nationally, see *Approaching Equality of Opportunity in Higher Education,* in Francis J. Brown (ed.), American Council on Education Studies, Reports of Committees and Conferences, ser. 1, vol. 19, no. 59, Washington, D.C., 1955, *passim.* For a clear statement of the difference between equal opportunity and increased opportunity, see Ernest Van Den Haag, *Education as an Industry,* Augustus M. Kelley, Inc., New York, 1956, pp. 39–40.

place for the potential dropout. This implication has been recognized and advocated, by some junior college supporters:[3]

> At present over the nation, 50 per cent of our entering students drop out of college during the first two years, and only 35 to 40 per cent are graduated. Most of these dropouts are predestined to fail and can be identified before they enter. Their presence creates difficult problems for college faculties. They could be much better served in local community colleges, and at much less cost.

Willing or not, the junior college must assume this role which is intrinsic to its character and place. But the role does not lend itself to a popular definition; too often it will lead outsiders to see in the junior college a place for third-rate students—the culls of other colleges. This perception has strong negative consequences for the status of the college in society. Junior college staffs themselves are reluctant to embrace such a definition, and it remains a troublesome point in the identity and status of junior colleges.

These performances of widening college admission and screening students lead to another consideration. The latent terminal student, as described earlier, aspires to transfer to another college to complete four years, but is destined never to get past the junior college. The number of such students is large in the junior college, as is the number of short-term students in American higher education generally. Handling latent terminal or short-term students is an important educational problem with wide social implications. The performance that is entailed may be called the "cooling-out function."[4] The situation that makes

[3] James A. Starrak and Raymond M. Hughes, *The Community College in the United States*, Iowa State University Press, Ames, Iowa, 1954, p. 5.

[4] The analysis of this social function borrows from the work of Erving Goffman, on the ways in which the disappointing of expectations is handled by the disappointed person and especially by those responsible for the disappointment. Although Goffman based his formulation chiefly on the confidence

this function necessary and the operation of the function itself may be described in terms of a broad disjunction between ends and means in education.[5]

There are several sources of a build-up of a "must go to college" orientation in American youth. The general emphasis in our culture on individual achievement excites a pressing-on through education, because it is now apparently widely perceived that a college education is the main road to upward mobility. For an increasing number of professional, business, and scientific fields, college is the normal gateway. Aspirations of students, supported by the hopes of their parents, build a general pressure for higher education.[6] Besides, the "equal rights" beliefs of a general democratic ethos become readily translated, as previously indicated, into a doctrine that all have a right to enter college.

Thus the aspirations of the latent terminal student are encouraged and sustained by general premises of our culture. The

---

game, where facts are deliberately misrepresented to the "mark" by operators, the general notion of a cooling-out function can be applied as well to situations of failure in which those responsible act in good faith. See "On Cooling the Mark Out: Some Aspects of Adaptations to Failure," *Psychiatry,* vol. 15, no. 4, pp. 451–463, November, 1952. The general relevance of the Goffman conception to the situation analyzed here was suggested by Sheldon Messinger.

[5] For a general discussion of the possibility of disjuncture between cultural goals and institutional means, see Robert K. Merton, *Social Theory and Social Structure,* revised and enlarged ed., Free Press, Glencoe, Ill., 1957, pp. 132–139.

[6] One researcher has commented on the basis of lengthy, exploratory interviews in a remote farming community of Colorado in 1957 that subsistence farmers and skilled workingmen alike believe that their own lack of education proved to be a barrier. "The majority have drawn the moral that their sons are going to college, or beyond, come hell or high water. Not a few of them have succeeded in getting their sons to college." With this personal meaning of a college education, free college education and student subsidy may readily become "the present-day equivalent of the Homestead Act." Stephen T. Boggs, in personal communication.

student is attached to culturally prescribed ends that persuade him that he should go as far as possible and amount to something. The open-door policy encourages this belief and supports the sentiment that going to college is a right. But the achievement of college-related goals is another matter, because the means of achievement are not necessarily closely attuned to these ends. The means may be imperfectly formed, and they are especially likely to be conditioned by other ends. High standards is one such end in higher education (economy of resources is another). While a democratic ethos may set personal ends, the standards of higher education control the means. This is the general value conflict behind the situation of the latent terminal student. The standards of higher education do not allow him to proceed past the thirteenth or fourteenth year, and he is thus over-aspiring.

This may be seen, then, as a situation of structured failure. The disjuncture between ends and means, between the open door and standards, dooms large numbers of students to failure. A basic need is thus created in higher education, the need of knowing how to handle the induced failures. This need exists in varying degrees of intensity in different states according to (1) the magnitude and strength of the social pressure for college entry and (2) the concern for quality and high standards. When both are high, a potentially explosive situation exists for the public colleges. What is to be done when the pressure on colleges from the state legislators, city officials, parents, and students is to open wide the doors, but when, at the same time, college staffs and some outside groups are determined to hold up and possibly raise the standards of admission and attainment?

One answer is to have an essentially unselective state university. Such a university bows to the social pressure for broad admission but then generally attempts to protect standards by internal devices. Basically, this means a considerable effort to reduce enrollment sharply by the end of the first year. The college in part adopts the attitude, We have to let them in but we don't have to keep them; and the first year is used to weed out those that the staff define as incompetent.

Another answer is to have the junior college available to face the multitude with the open door, while the other public colleges select students. The junior college in effect is asked to cool out the incompetent. As was seen in the discussion of the latent terminal student in San Jose Junior College, this function is not easy to perform and requires various devices. The latent terminal student is allowed into transfer curricula but encounters counseling and testing that invite him to consider alternatives, subtle pressures to hedge his bet by taking courses that serve a terminal destiny, tough talk in orientation classes about realistic occupational choice, probationary status perhaps, and finally grades that will not allow transferring. He can be let down gradually, in what can be interpreted as a process of gentle stalling. As remarked by Goffman in another context: "He is given a chance to become familiar with the new conception of self he will have to accept before he is absolutely sure that he will have to accept it." [7] The student also moves through a funnel, with various persons and devices gradually narrowing his movement. He is asked early to consider possible failure in his attempt at a prolonged college education. Later he is tapered out.

The innovation of the junior college in performing the cooling-out function is providing structured alternatives. When a first-year student fails in the state university, he must remove himself from the institution and the premises. The failing occurs in a sense, in public, often with the student returning to his home. This may be dangerous for a university when hundreds and thousands of students are affected, because outsiders may

[7] A general description provided by Goffman on the stalling procedure for cooling out the disappointed person. Goffman, *op. cit.,* p. 458.

view the practice as a ruthless and heartless elimination, amounting to a slaughter of the innocents.[8] A university may not be able to keep this practice up indefinitely. In the junior college, the student does not so clearly fail, unless he himself wishes to define it that way, but rather transfers to terminal work. He may then interpret the second choice as more appropriate to his particular talent and be less frustrated that his first intention did not work out. The terminal student can be made to appear not so radically different from the transfer student, e.g., an "engineering aide" instead of "engineer," and hence he goes to something with a status of its own.[9] This reflects less unfavorably on a person's capacities. The junior college also provides a staff that is more oriented toward consoling the latent terminal student than would be the case in the state university. The junior college teacher-counselor practices the art of consolation.

The role of the junior college in assuming this function promises to be more important nationally in the decades ahead. The demand for college admission is expanding rapidly because of larger high school graduating classes and a larger percentage of these graduates going on to college. Even if standards were held constant in baccalaureate colleges, a larger number of students would probably need to be turned away or failed in the future than at present, because the size of the physical plant alone will impose some limitation or at least a lag in capacity. But many attempts are being made to raise admission requirements and standards of retention rather than to maintain them at present levels or lower them. Heavy demand gives many colleges an opportunity to escape former limitations of clientele and be-

[8] Robert L. Kelly, *The American Colleges and the Social Order,* The Macmillan Company, New York, 1940, pp. 220–221.

[9] "A . . . general solution to the problem of cooling the mark out consists of offering him a status which differs from the one he has lost or failed to gain but which provides at least a something or a somebody for him to become." Goffman, *op. cit.,* p. 457.

come more selective. It may be anticipated that the situation will become more explosive in most states, deepening the need for the cooling-out function. The character of the locally controlled, comprehensive junior college renders it a suitable instrument for this function.

A dilemma of this role, however, is that it needs to remain reasonably latent, not clearly perceived and understood by prospective clientele. Should the function become obvious, the ability of the junior college to perform it would be impaired. The realization that the junior college is a place where students reach undesired destinations would turn the pressure for college admission back on the "protected" colleges. The widespread identification of the junior college as principally a transfer station, aided by the ambiguity of the "community college" label, helps to keep this role reasonably opaque to public scrutiny.

The performances of screening students for other colleges and handling latent terminal students suggest that the junior college is an agency in higher education which supplements and protects the work of other colleges. This is true, but not in the sense that the junior college is merely a passive appendage. As the role of the unselective college is structured in California and elsewhere when the public junior college is locally controlled, its place and character effect a reorganization of higher education. The first two years of college become separated from the baccalaureate centers and are made a part of secondary education. This is not merely a legal shift, as has been seen. The freshman and sophomore college student (the "pure transfer" type in the junior college) takes his education with "noncollege" (pure and latent terminal) students in a school that must orient itself in part to the needs of the latter. The organizational and curricular setting thus given to the freshman and sophomore years is unlike that of previous locations and is similar to the comprehensive high school.

This reorganization is little discussed and apparently not

readily perceived. Since the name of "college" connotes an agency that is not secondary, the shift in place and focus may be easily missed. At the same time, this reorganization is in line with the expressed hopes of early advocates of the junior college. President W. R. Harper, of the University of Chicago, near the turn of the century held that "the work of the freshman and sophomore years in the colleges of this country . . . is but a continuation of the academy or high-school work," and on this basis he favored the development of high schools into junior colleges.[10] An early advocate of the comprehensive junior college, Dean Alexis F. Lange, of the University of California, repeatedly depicted the junior college as "an organic part of a high school full-grown," and saw this "upward extension of the high school" as related to "the educational interest of the great mass of high-school students, who cannot, will not, should not become university students."[11] This advocated change in the location and orientation of the first two college years is now taking place gradually and quietly by means of such schools as San Jose Junior College.

This reorganization carries with it an upward extension of the authority of the public schools, which is a development that may be seen as another aspect of a democratization trend. The junior college not only extends student opportunity, but also lifts the control of local public school officials from the former ceiling of grade 12 to a new high of grade 14, or the junior year of college. In so doing, it extends local influence on education generally. The first two years of college move from control structures that are relatively independent of local influence to

[10] William Rainey Harper, *The Trend in Higher Education,* University of Chicago Press, Chicago, 1905, pp. 83, 382–383. A similar view was held by President Jordan of Stanford University.

[11] Jesse P. Bogue, *The Community College,* McGraw-Hill Book Company, Inc., New York, 1950, p. 345.

administrative systems that are dependent on the local community.[12]

This reorganization has been favored in California by leading officials of the state university.[13] For the interests of a state university, the public junior college is clearly protective. The former president of the University of California has maintained [14] that:

> Without the excellent junior colleges that have been developed, [the University of California] would hardly have been able to establish and maintain its present high standards of admission and graduation, as would also have been true had there been no state colleges. Certainly class size could not have been held to a reasonable level, nor could the need for land and buildings have been kept within bounds.

The quality of advanced programs is served by having within the state a type of college dedicated to absorbing lower-division students in whatever numbers they appear. The branches of the university are saved from contending with even larger student bodies than they now have, and are somewhat protected against demands for a less selective admission policy. A gradual loss of control over the first two years of college education has apparently not been too great a price to pay for these advantages, especially since the university has its own relatively small lower division against which to measure the transfer students.

Taken together, these aspects of role indicate a basic interpretation of the public junior college. An important effect of the unselective college is to permit a system of higher education as a whole to be both "democratic" and selective. All can go to col-

[12] For another discussion of this change, see David Riesman, *Constraint and Variety in American Education*, University of Nebraska Press, Lincoln, Nebr., 1956, pp. 122–123.

[13] For example, see Robert Gordon Sproul, "Many Millions More," *The Educational Record*, vol. 39, no. 2, pp. 97–103, April, 1958.

[14] *Ibid.*, p. 101.

lege, with participation differentiated among agencies that vary from highly selective to nonselective. The junior college makes this fully possible.

PROBLEMS OF CHARACTER AND ROLE

The central dilemma of character faced by San Jose Junior College, and held in common with other public junior colleges, can be posed in educational terms as follows: How can an educational organization be both a public school and a college? The major hiatus in the organization and outlook of American education has been between the secondary school and the college. In straddling this divide, the public junior college meets contradictions that are not readily resolved. The dilemma, as seen in San Jose, has at least three aspects: problems of status, identity, and autonomy.

The Problem of Status

A public school that attempts to parallel, in part, the work of the university and the four-year college cannot escape comparison with these agencies. Its lower-division work renders the junior college a part of higher education, to be judged by criteria of this realm. The name of "college" alone, as David Riesman has suggested, tends to place an organization in this higher league.[15] But the images and standards of higher education are not kind to the junior college. The status of college organizations in the general society flows in a large measure from academic prominence and influence. The type of degree offered is a primary factor, with a gradation of status from the Ph.D. to the M.A., the B.A., and finally to the two-year A.A. degree. The amount of work required and the status attached produces an

[15] See David Riesman, "Secondary Education and 'Counter-cyclical' Policy," *Constraint and Variety in American Education*, University of Nebraska Press, Lincoln, Nebr., 1956, pp. 107–110.

assumption that two-year programs are basically of a lower order than four-year ones. The two-year degree in fact has little standing. The training and reputation of the faculty is another basis for assigning status, high value being given to the nationally known scholar. Here the junior college is almost completely out of the race. Similarly, the public junior college is poorly ranked when judged by academic selectivity of student body. On many grounds it is easy for the junior college to be defined as a second- or third-rate college.

The decisive feature in the assignment of status to types of colleges is probably their relationship to occupations. The university prepares students in its professional and graduate schools for occupations of high social status, such as the established professions, science, business management; the four- or five-year college relates directly to occupations of somewhat lower status for the most part, in which neither advanced graduate nor prolonged professional school training is needed, such as teaching, engineering, lower management positions in business and goverment. The junior college, in turn, prepares semiprofessionals and technicians. The differential status of these occupations inevitably attaches to the preparatory agencies. As has been observed in the relationship of education to occupations in Britain,[16] it is unrealistic to expect equality of status for schools when they are differentially related to an outside hierarchy of social status. Thus, to the extent that the terminal work of the junior college is perceived, the link between education and the social status of occupations means an organizational standing below other major forms of college organization.

Within the general limits of a tertiary status in higher education, below that of the university and four-year college, a junior college enters into status competition with others of its kind. The California junior colleges assess themselves informally

[16] Olive Banks, *Parity and Prestige in English Secondary Education*, Routledge & Kegan Paul, Ltd., London, 1955, chap. 16.

and are ranked by others officially and unofficially, in comparison with one another. Here status leverage is available to the individual junior college. The interests of the university and four-year colleges lie almost solely in the transfer students. In addition, many outsiders perceive the junior college only in terms of the quality of its transfer output, having identified it in their own minds as principally a decentralized lower division. Viewed then as a feeder college, the success of the transfer students becomes important in academic standing. San Jose Junior College had already become concerned, by the end of four years, with the grade-point averages attained by the relatively few students who transferred to the University of California, because in its close attention to grade-point differentials, the university soon has in its own terms the measure of a junior college. Academic status as a feeder college thus calls for the nurturing and close control of actual transfers, and presses for attention to the more academic aspects of work.

Academic status affects the standing of a junior college in the local community but by no means completely determines it. The status ascribed by local laymen is based in part on their own ranking of academic programs and their understanding of academic respectability. In San Jose, the common view that the junior college is a home for state-college rejects lowers its status. But as also seen, status can be affected by cost of program and displacement of established schools. Judgment on such bases is shaped by traditional premises of what various types of schools do. Well-established in the common and professional conceptions of American education is the break between the public school and the college. A new junior college finds the expectations traditional to each of these to be ill-fitting. When the college is seen as just another public school, expectations on cost, personnel, and students tend to parallel those applied to the high school. When viewed as a college alone, it is judged in terms traditional to colleges. From either side, the unique characteristics of the junior college, as its advocates say, are misunderstood.

A secure status for a junior college, in this way, finally depends largely on perception of it as something different and acceptance of this difference. A recognition reasonably consonant with the character of the junior college thus seems dependent on the building and communicating of an identity. Such a college needs to spread the word locally about much of the particular combination of tasks and roles it has assumed. An identity also needs to be shown to the college world. This suggests that the building of a communicable and socially acceptable identity is *the* problem resulting from the character of the unselective junior college.

The Problem of Identity

An effort, then, to sell a new junior college to outsiders and to achieve a secure status in the general society is likely to be successful if the organization has a sense of identity and communicates it in acceptable terms. The first requirement, the building of a somewhat distinctive image, is made difficult for the public junior college, however, by its overlap with better-known types of schools. Duplication in one direction lies in its role as a lower division for senior colleges and universities. As seen in San Jose, in addition, there may also be a jurisdictional overlap with technical high schools and adult programs. When asked to assume programs formerly conducted by regular high schools, there is additional confusion. The gaining of a reasonably clear identity is further complicated by the interplay of conflicting needs and orientations. The need of the junior college for status in the academic world pulls orientation toward transfer work; but the need for a unique function, to be able to do something that no other organization does, pulls toward the terminal, as does the noncollege nature of the majority of the student body. The uniqueness of the terminal work is of special value, at first glance, in building and projecting an identity, since a unique operation can be used to claim a distinctive place in education. But since diffuse commitment is a central aspect of character, the claim of unique function tends to become submerged and blurred in with other functions. Needed in the comprehensive college are self-conceptions and educational formulae that embrace and rationalize diverse programs. Busy with problems of organization, San Jose Junior College had barely begun in its early years to elaborate a doctrinal definition of its place in the world. Its personnel had only lately turned to the creation of an image of the institution as a community college,[17] a concept now forwarded by many junior colleges in attempting to achieve a viable identity. The construction of this image requires that it be understood, accepted, and assimilated by the personnel of the college and then explained to outsiders. Short on self-image, the college's problem of projecting an identity to and beyond the community remained basically unsolved.

In general, the extent to which the community college definition of the junior college can provide an organizational identity, in San Jose and elsewhere, is problematic. It carries prestige as a self-conception for a local school. It fits the primary conditions of existence for the public junior college—that it is locally controlled and supported. The conception has a "folk halo" useful for local acceptance. At the same time, junior college administrators find it difficult to convince their own personnel, let alone outsiders, to absorb this image to the point where it changes attitudes and expectations. There are connotations attached to the word "college" that are slow to change, remaining relatively un-

[17] In its fifth year, the college was renamed San Jose City College, a title that omits the word "junior" and more closely suggests a college that services the local area. A major unpublished report prepared by the college in its fifth year placed the general objectives of the college as those of a community college.

affected in the minds of teachers and the public by new terms and symbols. One of these attached meanings is that the quality of any agency claiming to be a college is to be judged by the brightness of its students and the standards of its staff. This belief, supported by academic tradition and the status rewards of quality, would appear to be constantly at work undercutting a diffuse, comprehensive image.

A college that is basically a secondary school remains confusing to many. The principal administrative answer in San Jose and elsewhere to the constant reasserting of the older image of college appears to be the recruitment of personnel from "below." High school teachers and administrators understand the characteristics of secondary education, providing a more acceptable internal base on which to build a community college conception. Teachers and administrators bred to traditional college cultures, on the other hand, are usually impatient or confused, claiming that such a conception is watering down and corrupting higher education. But even where the more acceptable base for a community college image is built within the college by the recruiting of secondary-school personnel, it may be anticipated that the problem of identity will persist to a considerable degree. The diffusion in commitment that is part of the character of the comprehensive junior college leads to a certain amount of attenuation and confusion.[18] In an organization with numerous broad purposes it is much more difficult to know specifically what the enterprise is about than in specialized agencies. Even such widely accepted, secure public institutions as the American high school find themselves plagued with the problem of identity. For new organizations in less secure, ill-defined realms, the problem is acute.

It was earlier pointed out that an important role of the junior

[18] For a discussion of attenuated and confused organization character, see Philip Selznick, *The Organizational Weapon*, McGraw-Hill Book Company, Inc., New York, 1952, pp. 144–145.

college is its cooling-out function in higher education and that a dilemma of this role is that it needs to remain latent. This dilemma plays a decisive part in the identity problem. Accurate self-assessment by a junior college staff will see that cooling out is an important function of the college. Yet it is largely unacceptable as part of a self-image and almost completely so as a public image. Is the junior college to advertise that one of its major tasks is to remove from higher education those students who should not be there according to the standards of other colleges? This is sharply put, to pose clearly the identity problem. Junior college staffs need to understand this role in order to grasp fully what their organizations' business is; at the same time, it is against organizational self-interest to communicate this part of a total image. This difficulty highlights the practical value of a community college conception; its organizational function is to be a general screen behind which unnamed and unperceived tasks are performed.[19]

The Problem of Autonomy

Status and identity may well be common problems of mass organizations, especially in realms where "nonmass" expectations are dominant. Such organizations also face problems of independence of action. One aspect of the San Jose situation was the college's administrative dependence, a feature intrinsic to unified management of a larger system. This sharply limited the freedom of the college to seek and develop its own potentialities. By this dependency such values as simplicity and integration of authority in the public schools as a whole were served. But poorly served was organizational self-determination, and the unified college clearly faces this as a special problem.

[19] It is not to be inferred from this that the junior college is especially guilty of masking its work. Organizations attempt to present a favorable image to the outside world, and various ideologies and conceptions are used to rationalize and cover organizational practices.

More important, however, is the dependency highlighted in this report. The mass college is characteristically vulnerable to unorganized influences that, while hidden from easy identification, are persistently character-shaping. The bridge over which these influences flow is the dependent relationship to unselected clients. The people-processing institution is very close to its social base, and central to its making is its *mode of definition* of clientele. The style reflected in the San Jose case is nearly a nondefinition, because in its acceptance of all, the organization leaves the specific make-up of its clientele to individual choice. The public junior college does not actually define a clientele, but receives a self-constituted one.

This admission style makes the public junior college a vulnerable organization, easily reached and affected by trends of interest in the local community. In California this feature was in effect decreed for the junior college by state law. Once established, it has come to be interpreted as a virtue in conceptions of service to the local community. But as an operational fact, this condition sharply limits the extent to which an organization can consciously determine itself. In its lack of autonomy, the open-door college has the definition of character taken away from planning and professional control and diffused to external sources. Thus we find a type of formal organization determined to a large degree by context and hence to be explained largely in terms of sociological determinism. Institutional leadership is minimized, and direction by context, maximized. Along a continuum of organizational power in environmental relations, ranging from the organization that dominates its environmental relations to one completely dominated by its environment, the public junior college tends strongly toward the latter extreme.[20]

[20] For a discussion of this continuum, see James D. Thompson and William J. McEwen, "Organizational Goals and Environment: Goal-setting as an Interaction Process," *American Sociological Review,* vol. 23, no. 1, pp. 23–31, especially p. 25, February, 1958.

Like state universities and state colleges, junior colleges can somewhat diminish their vulnerability by internal devices. All students must be admitted, but then they can be differentially treated; for example, criteria for admission to various programs can be established, to control better the impact of students on the program structure. But the foremost issue in the control of a constituency is who is to have access to membership. The mass college will elaborate internal processing devices precisely to gain some self-direction, but the basic source of the problem of autonomy remains. The power to select a social base is to be seen as the ultimate variable in the determination of the character of the public two-year college. To select or not to select is finally the critical decision.

APPENDIXES

APPENDIX I

Methodological Note

As a study of an organization, this investigation focused on large social units. It was not designed to describe individual participants or small groups, but an organization and its context. This focus needs to be kept in mind, for it may be overlooked in considering the separate parts of this report. Both the research and the analysis necessarily had to proceed bit by bit and aspects of the whole had to be distinguished from one another. The study analytically separated, for example, the job requirements of the teacher, the orientation of the administrative staff, and the aptitude of the students. In reporting on such topics, the level of analysis may at times seem to have shifted from the organization as a whole to component units. But the point of the more detailed analysis was to report features that may be seen as attributes of the total organization. Thus the ability of the student was considered as the aggregate ability of a student body, which may be seen as an attribute of the organization. It also needs to be said that the several arrays of numerical data presented in this study take their meaning from their bearing on a single case rather than on a number of instances. The teacher survey, for example, was taken as part of the internal analysis of one case, the college as a whole, rather than as the extensive review that is normally exhibited by a survey. The study was a case study throughout.[1]

The research was almost entirely carried out by informal means—by unstructured interview and observation and the perusal of documents. In an exploratory phase of the project, interviews were held with more than a dozen junior college administrators in northern California to locate an organization promising and convenient for study and to gain some insight and understanding of practices and problems of junior colleges. After intensive work began in San Jose in the latter part of 1955, informal discussions were held with administrative personnel of the headquarters of the San Jose Unified School District, with administrators of the San Jose Junior College, and with approximately one-fourth of the college's teaching staff. The interviewing was most comprehensive with the administrators of the college. These interviews lasted from one to three hours and the administrators were reinterviewed over a two-year period; in several cases, the reinterviewing took up to a dozen visits. The material produced by interviewing in this manner was a somewhat disordered aggregation of relevant and irrelevant material, of hard facts and undependable assertions. But by this means, a rich fund of information was accumulated, and convergences in the reporting of facts and interpretation between a few knowledgeable respondents produced several of the guide lines of the study. Interviewing was the basic source of information on the place of the college in the district, for example. At the same time, however, every effort was made to avoid dependence on hearsay. Interview information used in this study was cross-checked among respondents and especially was checked against information found in documents. In the final writing, the attempt was made to base analysis on documentary evidence, pub-

[1] On the merits of single-case analysis versus extensive comparative analysis, see Seymour M. Lipset, M. Trow, and J. Coleman, *Union Democracy,* Free Press, Glencoe, Ill., 1956, pp. 425–427.

lic reports in most cases, or survey results; rarely was it necessary to use the undocumented response of a single person.

Records and memoranda became in this study the primary source of dependable material, as well as a check on interview results. The documentation of Chapter 1 was derived from an exhaustive review of school-board minutes from 1921 to 1957, a perusal of available policy memoranda, and a study of state reports and newspaper accounts. The comparative analysis of four colleges in Chapter 2 was similarly based on existing records, as was nearly all the rest of this chapter. For specific detail or broad policy, existing written accounts were *the* source, and the accounts generally had the last word when several sources gave contradictory results. This point is emphasized here because files have had little status in sociology as a research source. Actually their role in organizational study may be a primary one.

Formal methods of research played only a minor role in this study. One formal device was used, a mail questionnaire sent to the professional staff of the college in the fall of 1957. This questionnaire had the special advantage of allowing some of the results from San Jose Junior College to be compared with those of a national survey. But it was, in fact, a late appendage to the study, and the basic interpretation of the character of the college was derived before the survey results were available. Hence the study relied almost completely on more informal methods. The informal procedures permitted intensive work with selected sources. To ask about the determinants of a particular policy, it is more promising to go to the five persons likely to know than to fifty that do not know. The formal means of gathering information lean heavily on the awareness and level of information of a relatively large number of respondents. At the same time, much about the character of an organization may be little known or only dimly perceived by the typical participant, and the determinants and consequences of character are particularly removed from the view of many. The participant is involved with the specific tasks at hand and is likely to have had little reason to assume the stance of a historian or an analyst. It is also to be assumed at the outset of an institutional study that some of the major internal changes and external adaptations of an organization may be beyond the awareness of all participants, that *latent* tendencies and functions may be identified by the outsider who comes at the organization with a particular analytical point of view. The hope of saying something new and useful rests on such an assumption. While formal techniques can contribute to this quest in organizational studies of the level and type represented here, they can hardly be relied upon as the sole or perhaps even the major source of significant information.

The questionnaire used in this study was mailed to the staff of San Jose Junior College at the same time (fall, 1957) that it was sent to the staffs of seventy-four other junior colleges and university extension centers by the Center for the Study of Higher Education, University of California (Berkeley).[2] The respondents to the survey totaled more than 3,200. For San Jose, 102 questionnaires were mailed out and 90, or 88 per cent, were returned completed. The San Jose questionnaires were separately analyzed, to provide relevant information for this case study. At the same time, the opportunity was taken at several points to compare the case data with results of the national survey. The questionnaire contained some items of little pertinence to the case study, such as the political preferences of junior college teachers, and only selected items were analyzed for the staff of San Jose Junior College. The most useful questions were reported at several places in the body of this report. Because of its limited relevance, the questionnaire is not reproduced here; it will be available in later studies, and copies may be obtained from the Center.

[2] See Leland L. Medsker, *The Junior College: Progress and Prospect*, McGraw-Hill Book Company, Inc., New York, 1960, chap. 7.

APPENDIX 2

Socioeconomic Analysis

The four-college comparison reported in Chapter 2 was made by means of two indicators of student background. One was the occupation of father and the other, the socioeconomic nature of the neighborhood in which the student's family resided. The first index was simple enough, requiring only the occupation of father as reported by the individual student (a "personal variable") and a categorizing of occupations by socioeconomic level. The second indicator was more complex, because neighborhoods had to be characterized and their scores then assigned to students (a "unit variable").[1] Ordinarily this would be difficult, but a typology designed for the analysis of social areas of cities, constructed by Shevky and Bell,[2] had previously been worked out for the city of San Jose,[3] on the basis of 1950 census

[1] On personal and unit variables, and the use of unit data to characterize individuals, see Patricia L. Kendall and Paul F. Lazarsfeld, "Problems of Survey Analysis," in Robert K. Merton and Paul F. Lazarsfeld (eds.), *Continuities in Social Research: Studies in the Scope and Method of "The American Soldier,"* Free Press, Glencoe, Ill., 1950, pp. 187–196.

[2] Eshref Shevky and Wendell Bell, *Social Area Analysis*, Stanford University Press, Stanford, Calif., 1955.

[3] Stephen T. Boggs, "Social Areas of San Jose," unpublished manuscript.

data; hence characterizations of areas of the city were readily available. A college student could be placed in this typology, and several kinds of scores derived for him, by simply ascertaining the census tract in which his family lived and assigning tract scores to him.

Thus altogether only two facts on each student were needed, father's occupation and the San Jose street address of family residence. This information was sought from college records for students entering four colleges from the city of San Jose in the academic year 1955–1956. Stanford University and the University of California at Berkeley, however, proved to have few San Jose entrants (approximately fifteen a year at Stanford and twenty-five a year at Berkeley), and the number of cases was increased by using entering students for the previous four years. For San Jose State College, information was obtained on all entrants from San Jose for the year 1955–1956, and for San Jose Junior College, a 50 per cent sample of the 1955–1956 entrants was taken by using every other name in an alphabetical listing. Cases were lost in all four colleges for various reasons. Important among these were incomplete information in the records on father's occupation and unusable information on street addresses. The home addresses of San Jose students had to be located in census tracts whose characteristics were reported in the 1950 census. Many addresses could not be located and scored because they were in areas of the city annexed since 1950. These areas were principally suburban upper-middle-class neighborhoods and hence the cases finally used underrepresented this segment of the 1956 city population. The "old" San Jose of 1950 was, in effect, the base line of the four-college comparison.

The occupational categories shown in Tables 5, 6, and 7 in Chapter 2 were defined as follows: as "upper-white-collar," professionals, managers, proprietors, and officials; "lower-white-collar," sales, clerical, and kindred workers; "upper-blue-collar," craftsmen, foremen, and operatives; and "lower-blue-collar," service workers and laborers. The categories of neighborhood economic status used in Table 8 were derived in the following way: all fifty-nine census tracts of the city of San Jose shown in the 1950 census were given scores on the economic status (or "social rank") dimension of the Shevky-Bell typology. This variable is composed of measures of occupation and education for entire tract populations.[4] The tracts of the city ranged from 28 to 85 in economic-status scores, on a theoretically possible scale of 0 to 100. To arrive at four categories of economic status, the San Jose range of nearly sixty units was divided into four equal parts as follows: "high," 85 to 70; "medium high," 69.9 to 55; "medium low," 54.9 to 40; and "low," 39.9 to 25. The number of tracts that fell in each category was fifteen, seventeen, fifteen, and twelve. A four-part split was made in order to have the same number of categories as for father's occupation. As can be seen by comparing Tables 5 and 8, these two indicators of the student's socioeconomic background offer essentially the same comparison of the four colleges, with San Jose Junior College in each case closely approximating the city-wide distribution. Students were also jointly classified by the father's occupation and economic status of neighborhood, as shown in the following table. Here the father's occupation was divided into two categories, white collar and blue collar; neighborhood status was also divided, with high status incorporating the previous "high" and "medium high" categories (scores of 55 to 85) and low status covering the previous "medium low" and "low" categories (scores of 25 to 54.9). A fourfold classification for each college was used mainly because of the low number of cases. Table 21 suggests several points: the highly selective and relatively expensive colleges (Stanford and the University of California) receive few students from low-status neighborhoods of the city; when students do come from such neighborhoods, they are likely to have a white-collar father. These same colleges also receive

[4] For detailed explanation, see Shevky and Bell, *op. cit.*, pp. 54–55.

Table 21
Joint Classification of College Clientele by Father's Occupation and Economic Status of Neighborhood

College	White-collar occupation		Blue-collar occupation		Total
	High status neighborhood	Low status neighborhood	High status neighborhood	Low status neighborhood	
	Per cent	Per cent	Per cent	Per cent	
Stanford	82	13	5	0	100 (*N* = 55)
University of California	83	0	13	4	100 (N = 52)
San Jose State College	46	8	29	17	100 (*N* = 147)
San Jose Junior College	28	10	26	36	100 (*N* = 95)

SOURCES: College records and Stephen T. Boggs, "Social Areas of San Jose," unpublished manuscript.

few students from blue-collar families; when students do come from such a background, they are likely to be living in a high-status rather than low-status neighborhood. The maximum thrust toward these colleges, of course, is to have a white-collar family in a high-status neighborhood.

In contrast, San Jose State College received less than half (46.2 per cent) of its San Jose students from white-collar families in high-status neighborhoods, and San Jose Junior College showed 28.4 per cent of its students with such a background. At the other extreme of socioeconomic background, the State College was receiving 17 per cent of its students from the local city from blue-collar occupations in low-status neighborhoods, and the Junior College had more than a third of its students from the local city with this combination. (Stanford and the University of California receive virtually no students from such a background.)

The joint use of father's occupation and economic status of home neighborhood sharpens the picture of the differentiation of students among colleges, beyond using either index alone.

APPENDIX 3

A Note on Commitment

This study has pointed to the administrative setting of a college as a broad determinant of its character. This explanation is a kind of contextual analysis, an identification of important segments of the total matrix in which organizational action took place. At the same time, other major aspects of context were left aside. Larger social structures and cultural milieu, which in turn provide the context of the administrative setting and also affect the character of the college, were largely disregarded. The study provides little community analysis and treats only in passing of broad social forces and educational doctrines. This was done in part because the principal determinants of the college's character were seen to have stemmed directly from the nature of the administrative setting, the local school district, or else as having been brought to bear by it, as in the case of state admission requirements. The influence of local groups was also focused through this larger administrative unit, and explanation was possible without going far afield from the limits of this web of organization.

But there was also an additional reason for not examining the larger scene in more detail. The study avoided an extended analysis in order to emphasize all the more the often overlooked administrative context. In contextual analysis of schools and colleges, attention has tended to be drawn to influences completely external to the organizations at hand, for example, to local political forces, taxpayer groups, community sentiments, and the wishes of educationists. There is a very general tendency, for instance, to explain the public schools by saying that the community basically gets what it wants or that everything is decided by the educationists. The indeterminacy of such broad explanations is seldom explored, and the impact of organization itself—of the more immediate and more highly structured context—is played down. Yet the study of formal organizations is no less necessary to an understanding of educational affairs than it is to the work of the business firm or the government office. Patterns of action arise and change without direction by the community or educationists, but in response to specific internal and external pressures. "Drifts" set in, impelled by requirements of the organization as a system in its own right. Such phenomena can hardly be seen when the view is gross and external. The study of the outcomes of organized activity requires the study of organization.

In regard to current organizational analysis and theorizing, this study has an interesting implication. Organizational theory has for some time been centered on the notion of bureaucracy.[1] This concept has largely pointed to internal tendencies of organizations. It has drawn attention to the processes, rational and irrational, that are generated by an organization itself in the course

[1] The classic discussion of bureaucracy can be found in *From Max Weber: Essays in Sociology,* translated by H. H. Gerth and C. Wright Mills, Oxford University Press, New York, 1946, pp. 196ff. See also *Reader in Bureaucracy,* Robert K. Merton et al. (eds.), Free Press, Glencoe, Ill., 1952, and Peter M. Blau, *Bureaucracy in Modern Society,* Random House, Inc., New York, 1956.

of its work, e.g., the rational ordering of subunits, the routinization of work performances, and a growing rigidity of response. Broadly, the organization is seen as becoming tied to a certain character and role as routines set in and as internal and external alliances are formed. It has recently been suggested that organizational processes may be approached by means of a "theory of commitments," where a commitment of an organization is defined as "an enforced line of action." [2] These enforcements have been seen to stem largely from what the organization itself does during its life span. Commitments tend to accumulate as important decisions are made, and the organization moves from initial freedom to irrevocable patterns and ties. "Day-to-day decisions . . . create precedents, alliances, effective symbols, and personal loyalties." [3] The concept of commitment "indicates the ways in which present constraints are outcomes of earlier decisions and choices on the actors' part. This implies that the earlier choices were in some sense freer and possessed a greater variety of functional alternatives than did later ones." [4]

This view as well as that stemming directly from the concept of bureaucracy, it may be said, assumes for a large proportion of organizations too great a degree of initial innocence. A clean slate at the start may be too readily assumed if the context provided for an organization is not brought into view. Organizational theory needs to be accommodated to the fact that large classes of organizations start with their hands tied to a considerable degree, with the tying done by others who are part of the administrative context. In such cases, the primary commitments do not arise from processes internal to the suborganization itself

[2] Philip Selznick, *TVA and the Grass Roots*, University of California Press, Berkeley, Calif., 1949, pp. 255–259.

[3] *Ibid.*, p. 258.

[4] Alvin W. Gouldner, "Theoretical Requirements of the Applied Social Sciences," *American Sociological Review*, vol. 22, no. 1, p. 101, February, 1957.

or by decision of its own administrators. The interesting implication for bureaucratic theory is that if this is true, and it appears widely so among public schools and colleges, the early days of organization are not necessarily freer and more open to self-determination than later years. The earlier years are freer in the sense that internal routines have not yet become controlling, nor have consequences set in motion by one's own decisions come to roost. This is in line with bureaucratic theory, which emphasizes the settling-down of mature organizations. But earlier years may be less free than later ones, because the constraints imposed by others have more control in the beginning. The sequence in decision-making may be from working under premises set by others to working more on one's own terms as some authority is gained.

Thus while it is true that commitments grow as decisions are made, it need not follow that there is an inherent tendency toward reduction of discretion, for the hands of leaders to be tied by what they have done before. Organizations start out under widely varying degrees of freedom. For the many that begin under extensive constraint, one burden of leadership is to change the initial structure of commitments, shedding those influences, group ties, and lines of action that are unwanted and assuming those that aid in gaining a desired identity. While administrative discretion is reduced through time by bureaucratic tendencies, it may be enlarged by loosening the restraints present at the time of origin. The trend may be for the organization to become freer.

Thus, analysis of administrative settings, as a form of contextual analysis, may be instrumental in adding new dimensions to organizational theory. For any but the most independently based organizations, administrative context cannot be ignored. In time it should be possible to know the kinds of constraints that are typically a part of certain organizational positions and institutional locations.[5] For organizations that are part of a larger complex of organizations, such knowledge is an indispensable part of adequate explanation.

[5] For one condition that is widely found in organizations and that has predictable consequences, see the discussion of "organizational marginality" in Burton R. Clark, *Adult Education in Transition: A Study of Institutional Insecurity,* University of California Press, Berkeley, Calif., 1956, pp. 57–63, 148–150.

Bibliography

American Association of Junior Colleges: *Junior College Directory, 1957,* Washington, D.C.

American Council on Education: *Approaching Equality of Opportunity in Higher Education,* Francis G. Brown (ed.), American Council on Education Studies, Reports of Committees and Conferences, ser. 1, vol. 19, no. 59, Washington, D.C., 1955.

———: *American Junior Colleges,* 4th ed., Jesse P. Bogue (ed.), Washington, D.C., 1956.

Banks, Olive: *Parity and Prestige in English Secondary Education,* Routledge & Kegan Paul, Ltd., London, 1955.

Blau, Peter M.: *Bureaucracy in Modern Society,* Random House, Inc., New York, 1956.

Blegen, Theodore C.: *The Harvests of Knowledge: A Report on Research Potentials and Problems in the State University of New York,* The Research Foundation of State University of New York, Albany, N.Y., 1957.

Bogue, Jesse P.: *The Community College,* McGraw-Hill Book Company, Inc., New York, 1950.

California, State of: *A Report of a Survey of the Needs of California in Higher Education,* Committee on the Conduct of the Study of Higher Education in California, Sacramento, 1948.

———: *A Restudy of the Needs of California in Higher Education,* California State Department of Education, Sacramento, 1955.

———: Education Code, Sacramento, 1955.

———: *A Study of the Need for Additional Centers of Public Higher Education in California*, California State Department of Education, Sacramento, 1957.

———: *Apportionment of the State School Fund, Part I, Year Ending June 30, 1957*, California State Department of Education, Sacramento, 1957.

———: *A Study of Faculty Demand and Supply in California Higher Education, 1957–1970*, prepared for the Liaison Committee of the Regents of the University of California and the California State Board of Education, Berkeley and Sacramento, 1958.

California State Senate: *Twelfth Report, Senate Investigating Committee on Education*, S. Res. 168 (1953), 1955.

Clark, Burton R.: *Adult Education in Transition: A Study of Institutional Insecurity*, University of California Press, Berkeley, 1956.

Conant, James B.: *Education in a Divided World*, Harvard University Press, Cambridge, Mass., 1948.

Fretwell, Jr., Elbert K.: *Founding Public Junior Colleges*, Bureau of Publications, Teachers College, Columbia University, New York, 1954.

From Max Weber: Essays in Sociology, translated by H. H. Gerth and C. Wright Mills, Oxford University Press, New York, 1946.

Goffman, Erving: "On Cooling the Mark Out: Some Aspects of Adaptation to Failure," *Psychiatry*, vol. 15, no. 4, pp. 451–463, November, 1952.

Gouldner, Alvin W.: "Theoretical Requirements of the Applied Social Sciences," *American Sociological Review*, vol. 22, no. 1, pp. 92–102, February, 1957.

———: "Cosmopolitans and Locals: Toward an Analysis of Latent Social Roles, II," *Administrative Science Quarterly*, vol. 2, no. 4, pp. 444–480, March, 1958.

Harper, William Rainey: *The Trend in Higher Education*, University of Chicago Press, Chicago, 1905.

Hofstadter, Richard, and C. DeWitt Hardy: *The Development and Scope of Higher Education in the United States*, Columbia University Press, New York, 1952.

———, and Walter P. Metzger: *The Development of Academic Free-*

dom in The United States, Columbia University Press, New York, 1955.

Kelly, Robert L.: *The American Colleges and the Social Order,* The Macmillan Company, New York, 1940.

Lederer, Emil: *State of the Masses,* W. W. Norton & Company, Inc., New York, 1940.

Lipset, Seymour M., M. Trow, and J. Coleman: *Union Democracy,* Free Press, Glencoe, Ill., 1956.

Mannheim, Karl: *Man and Society in an Age of Reconstruction,* Harcourt, Brace and Company, Inc., New York, 1950.

Medsker, Leland L.: *The Junior College: Progress and Prospect,* McGraw-Hill Book Company, Inc., New York, 1960.

Merton, Robert K.: *Social Theory and Social Structure,* revised and enlarged ed., Free Press, Glencoe, Ill., 1957.

Merton, Robert K., et al. (eds.): *Reader in Bureaucracy,* Free Press, Glencoe, Ill., 1952.

Mills, C. Wright: *The Power Elite,* Oxford University Press, New York, 1956, chap. 13.

Mulligan, Raymond A.: "Socio-Economic Background and College Enrollment," *American Sociological Review,* vol. 16, no. 2, pp. 188–196, April, 1951.

The National Society for the Study of Education: "The Role of the Public Junior College," *The Public Junior College,* Fifty-fifth Yearbook, University of Chicago Press, Chicago, 1956, part 1.

Riesman, David: *The Lonely Crowd,* Yale University Press, New Haven, Conn., 1950.

———: *Constraint and Variety in American Education,* University of Nebraska Press, Lincoln, Nebr., 1956.

San Jose Junior College Announcements for 1953–1954, San Jose Unified School District, San Jose, 1953.

San Jose Junior College Bulletin, 1956–57, San Jose Unified School District, San Jose, 1956.

Selznick, Philip: *TVA and the Grass Roots,* University of California Press, Berkeley, Calif., 1949.

———: *The Organizational Weapon,* McGraw-Hill Book Company, Inc., New York, 1952.

———: *Leadership in Administration: A Sociological Interpretation,* Row, Peterson & Company, Evanston, Ill., 1957.

Shevky, Eshref, and Wendell Bell: *Social Area Analysis,* Stanford University Press, Stanford, Calif., 1955.

Spindt, H. A.: "Beginnings of the Junior College in California, 1907–1921," *College and University,* vol. 33, no. 1, pp. 22–28, fall, 1957.

Sproul, Robert Gordon: "Many Millions More," *The Educational Record,* vol. 39, no. 2, pp. 97–103, April, 1958.

Starrak, James A., and Raymond M. Hughes: *The Community College in the United States,* Iowa State University Press, Ames, Iowa, 1954.

Thompson, James D., and William J. McEwen: "Organizational Goals and Environment: Goal Setting as an Interaction Process," *American Sociological Review,* vol. 23, no. 1, pp. 23–31, February, 1958.

U.S. Bureau of the Census: *Census of Population: 1950,* vol. II, *Characteristics of the Population,* California, 1952, part 5.

U.S. Department of Health, Education, and Welfare: *Higher Education,* vol. 14, no. 5, January, 1958.

———: *Higher Education,* vol. 14, no. 7, March 1958.

Van Den Haag, Ernest: *Education as an Industry,* Augustus M. Kelly, Inc., New York, 1956.

Index